EATING
WITH THE
TUDORS

EATING WITH THE TUDORS

AN ILLUSTRATED HISTORY OF THE FOOD WITH RECIPES

BRIGITTE WEBSTER

PEN & SWORD **HISTORY**

AN IMPRINT OF PEN & SWORD BOOKS LTD.
YORKSHIRE – PHILADELPHIA

First published in Great Britain in 2023 by
PEN AND SWORD HISTORY
An imprint of
Pen & Sword Books Ltd
Yorkshire – Philadelphia

ISBN 978 1 39909 259 3

Typeset in Times New Roman 10.5/13.5 by
SJmagic DESIGN SERVICES, India.
Printed and bound in the UK by CPI Group (UK) Ltd.

Pen & Sword Books Limited incorporates the imprints of Atlas, Archaeology,
Aviation, Discovery, Family History, Fiction, History, Maritime, Military,
Military Classics, Politics, Select, Transport, True Crime, Air World, Frontline
Publishing, Leo Cooper, Remember When, Seaforth Publishing, The Praetorian
Press, Wharncliffe Local History, Wharncliffe Transport, Wharncliffe True Crime
and White Owl.

For a complete list of Pen & Sword titles please contact
PEN & SWORD BOOKS LIMITED
47 Church Street, Barnsley, South Yorkshire, S70 2AS, England
E-mail: enquiries@pen-and-sword.co.uk
Website: www.pen-and-sword.co.uk

Or

PEN AND SWORD BOOKS
1950 Lawrence Rd, Havertown, PA 19083, USA
E-mail: Uspen-and-sword@casematepublishers.com
Website: www.penandswordbooks.com

CONTENTS

ACKNOWLEDGEMENTS

The research for this book started a good decade ago and I am deeply grateful to every single person who has helped me with their encouragement in the writing of it. My wonderful family and friends have been the most willing guinea pigs in tasting hundreds of dishes prepared to ancient recipes.

I would also like to thank Heather Teysko, Dr Sarah Morris, Claire Ridgway, Cassidy Cash, Carol Ann Lloyd-Stanger and Janet Wertman for their ongoing support. My thanks also go to Johnna Holloway and Elise Fleming for having nurtured and guided me with their expertise on my path to this book.

I am very grateful to Diane Walker, Andy Cochrane and Terry Harris for having opened several closed doors for me.

I am deeply indebted to Laura Nuvoloni and the Earl of Leicester and the Trustees of the Holkham Estate for having given me access to study the unique, early recipe manuscript held in the library of the Earl of Leicester at Holkham Hall in Norfolk.

My thanks go to the NT, Exeter Cathedral and Norfolk Record Office for allowing me the use of their images. My deepest gratitude goes to all authors who I was able to reference throughout this book.

I am also very thankful to Professor Suzannah Lipscomb for having propelled me in front of her tour groups at Hampton Court to talk about Tudor food, and in doing so, shown me that there will always be an audience wishing to learn about such a niche subject, and for inviting me to talk about Tudor banqueting food on her podcast *Not just the Tudors* and her TV series *Walking Tudor England.*

Last but not least a huge thank you to Sarah-Beth Watkins for having recommended me to my publishers and for Pen & Sword for giving me the opportunity to share my work with all fans of Tudor history and keen cooks, as well as having provided me with the patient, empathetic and most supportive editor, Claire Hopkins.

PREFACE

The book you are holding is the one I wanted to buy several years ago and could not find: a cookery book specialising in Tudor food with both the original recipe and the modern version, together with a picture of each dish and relevant additional information on the history about the dishes themselves and their ingredients.

INTRODUCTION

Food and meals in Tudor England

Food history connects everything and we can strive to sketch a very general picture of food available in Tudor England through a number of documents such as cookery and recipe books, dietary books, paintings and other art forms, administrative documents, estate accounts, privy purse expenses, customs accounts, household accounts, chronicler descriptions, herbals, wills and probate inventories as well as travel accounts by foreigners who visited England.

We are indeed better informed about the eating habits of royalty and nobility, gentry and, during the second half of the sixteenth century, also the affluent and emerging middle class, but it is considerably more challenging to find relevant information and documents to tell us about the eating habits of the common people.

One of the most interesting facts about food in sixteenth-century England is just how much it changed from Henry VII to Elizabeth I. We can observe a change from the late medieval to the early modern in what was available and how they prepared it, and we can also witness a drastic change in attitude to what was considered a healthy, balanced diet.

The early part of Tudor England was culinarily much guided by Galen's theories and controlled by religious doctrine and a strict social hierarchy turning food into social markers. Feasting seems to follow fasting in ongoing repeats. Spices, dried fruit and meat were the order of the day and considered most desirable for English people of noble heritage. Food was being chosen on its merits to 'preserve' health, meaning that healthy people were advised to eat food that mirrored the qualities of their bodily humors. Only sick people – a case of your naturally balanced humors gone unbalanced – required a change of approach, and food with opposite qualities were needed to correct the imbalance.

According to Galen's principle, every person's body was made up of four humors: blood, phlegm, yellow bile (choler) and black bile (melancholy) Each one of these had qualitative properties that could be hot, cold, dry or moist, causing individual characters such as sanguine, phlegmatic, choleric and melancholic.

It was understood that all humans were born with a predominance of one particular humor, and age, gender, profession, country of residence, weather and season defined what diet and food you should stick to at any given time as food was also given appropriate humoral qualitative properties. The key to staying healthy was to match the right foods to your personal requirements: food was your 'corrective' or 'equaliser'. The use of vinegar, vegetables, fruit and spices meant that any potentially harmful food could be corrected, and the bad influence 'cancelled' – similar to saying now 'have an apple with your chocolate and the damage will be undone'. I'm sure you get the gist. The right cooking method could achieve the same, but more detailed examples will be given in the chapters to follow.

The latter part of the sixteenth century was dominated by food restrictions, imposed not by the church but through economic sanctions, society itself calling for more 'restraint', and food shortages caused by serious harvest failures. New food from various parts of the globe was beginning to be imported into England, triggering new fads.

Physicians and writers of health advice books were beginning to distance themselves from idealising courtly feasts and started to look into new ways of scientific analyses of the human body. People started to be influenced by the new medical treatments and theories provided by Paracelsus, a physician in Switzerland who made use of precious stones, metals, minerals and chemicals.

The result of this period was a number of essential oils distilled from minerals, spices and plants, as well as a general decline of spices used in cookery and a noticeable readiness to include more vegetables in the diet of the wealthy. Medieval taste started to rapidly lose favour and English cooks began to look at Italy and France for inspiration. Herbs were the new spices and English cookery adopted sugar for nearly everything. The general attitude taken by experts was changing and now the attitude was that all bodies needed constant correction in order to prevent illness. In other words, you were advised to always eat corrective food (food with opposite qualitative properties) even when you were feeling fine.

To the Tudors it was important to know how easily food was digested and passed through the body as it also indicated the level of nourishment it offered. People who led a physically active life, which was generally the lower, labouring class needed more solid and sustaining foods in contrast to the 'leisuring' upper class who needed lighter foods. In a time when the concept of calorie burning had not yet been discovered, the stomach and the whole process of digestion was seen as a cauldron which was cooking on a hot fire. Different foods needed different lengths of time to digest, and to allow to digest properly plenty of time was left between meals. Undigested food travelling through the digestive system half raw and uncooked was considered extremely dangerous, particularly to the brain.

Most English physicians in Tudor times agreed that the English, should have access to three meals a day as they lived in a cold climate. They stressed the importance of leaving at least four hours between dinner and supper and six hours between breakfast and dinner. Dinner should be taken about eleven before noon but 'a rich man when he will', and 'for a poore man when he may', says physician Thomas Cogan (1545-1607) in *The haven of health* in 1584. Between four and six hours after dinner is convenient to have supper, which is served about five in the universities, six o'clock in the country and in 'poore mens houses when leisure will serve', he states. For the question on how much one should eat at dinner, he advises to keep supper light and go by the English proverb 'after Supper walke a mile: or at the least wise, refraine from sleepe two or three houres'.[1]

Contemporary physician Thomas Muffet (1553-1604) declares in his book *Healths improvement* that 'breakfasts are fit for all men in stinking houses or close Cities, as also in the time of pestilence, and before you visit the sick'. People in the country are advised to skip breakfast. He also believed it is better to eat more at supper time but stresses to not 'gorge' oneself 'up to their gullet'. More common-sense recommendation follows in 'mince or chew your meat finely, eat leisurely,' and 'sit upright with your body for an hours space or less'. Sensibly, he states that a physician could not give advice on how long to sit at dinner, but mentions that the most honorable Peregine Lord Willoughby of Eresby took between seven and eight hours dining when he was in a rush.[2]

The order in which food was eaten at a meal mattered too. Pottage was best consumed first and cheese served at the end of a meal to help 'seal' the stomach, allowing the food to be properly cooked. Thomas Muffet complains that he utterly 'mislikes' the English custom to serve 'meats of hard concoction and less good nourishment served before pheasant and partridge' and advises that all 'light food of liquid and thin substance and easie of concoction' should be offered first.[3]

In Tudor England, food did not just maintain life and keep the body healthy and fit, it also signalled power, status and wealth to guests and the community by means of excess, pricey ingredients and rarity. Sumptuary legislation tried to control behaviour and consumption with the expressed intent to reduce waste and ostentation. Such laws limited what could be spent on weddings and other feasts and limited the amount of food served at each course. These campaigns against excess were partly a protest against gluttony but aimed to maintain social hierarchy.

In a very modern approach, people started to realise that perhaps fat people should eat more 'lean' food and thin people were advised to eat more fattening foods. The general consensus was to eat what is good for you rather than what tastes good. Surely, we can all relate to that message. I personally go by Elizabethan physician Thomas Cogan's reminder of his golden verse, '*Esse decet vivas, vivere non ut edas*' ('man feeds to live, and liveth not to feed').[4]

Food from the New World posed a dilemma for dietary writers as ascribing humors was tricky due to the lack of native food to compare it with, but a small number of foods from the Americas was almost instantly embraced: sugar, turkey and sweet potatoes showing the way.

Many estates were self-sufficient in food production, but most people obtained their food from weekly markets which generally provided everything the community needed. Some markets such as Stourbridge in Cambridgeshire specialised and attracted customers from all over England who wanted food supply for Lent and fish days. Cookery shops in towns provided 'fast food' for people without cooking facilities. These often sold low-quality, cheap pies as well as cooked meat, but also made ready sauces and confections for the wealthier client. Many were open all day and night – surprisingly modern. Taverns too provided ready meals but mostly for travelling people and the food was often of dubious quality.

Butchers sold mostly beef, pork, lamb and sausages; poultry was generally sold by women at the market. Bakers were necessary in every town and village as most people did not have their own bread oven. Most bakeries would allow local women to use their oven after they had finished baking the bread for the day. The wealthy had fresh bread every day, while the lower classes often ate stale bread in pottages. Bread along with ale and meat were the staple of all people in society. However, bread was also an identity marker and according to your status you would eat *manchet* bread (finest white wheat) if you were rich, *cheat* bread (wholemeal) was consumed by the majority and *maslin* bread (mixture of grains) by the working class. Fishmongers were a common sight in Tudor England and sold fresh, stock and salted fish.

Tudor recipes

Original Tudor recipes are a far cry from modern equivalents as their target audience was a very different one. Anybody who first glances at an original early Tudor recipe may be forgiven for abandoning the will to recreate an authentic dish as the text offers no list of clear ingredients, measurements or ordered approach of instructions. The spelling is often phonetic and generally influenced by local dialects making the whole project an even more daunting prospect.

These original recipes were more seen as an 'aide memoire' for cooks who did not require having the basics spelled out. Having cooking experience, therefore, helps in making recipes from the sixteenth century work. However, it needs to be stressed that often the lack of such information forces the cook to fill in the gaps, opening the text up to personal interpretation.

Original recipes display immense character and charm which gets lost in modern translation. This recipe book will give you both the original as well as my modern interpretation for you to be able to enjoy the recipe's charm and the modern clarification needed to make it a 'doable' task. I only give modern measurements where I deemed it necessary for the successful outcome, but generally I am encouraging the cook to be guided by their own intuition and taste as this will achieve a more authentic result then forcing my taste on the readers.

Specific Tudor measurements occurring in individual recipes are explained within the recipe to help get the proportions right. Furthermore, every recipe will provide you with additional, interesting information on either the dish itself or its main ingredients.

Tudor era food writers and authors of cookery books often shared the same recipes as plagiarism wasn't considered theft. I have recreated every single recipe in this book, some several times, from similar or even identical sources to pick out the one that was voted the best by my team of valuable 'food tasters' – family and friends, open-minded and happy to give an honest and objective verdict.

With each recipe I provide the original source, year of publication and the author, if known. I have also chosen to go with the original title with all its charm, but I am grateful to the publisher for allowing me to offer a photo of the final product to alleviate any confusion that might arise.

Tudor recipes are very much based on seasonal changes dictated by nature. This was the driving idea behind the choice of chapters, so you can cook through the seasons making use of native fresh produce in season – something we ought to be doing a lot more.

Tudor dishes and recipes never fail to surprise and amaze me, and in my years of recreating Tudor recipes I have only very occasionally not enjoyed what I have cooked. More often I found that a recipe which sounded less than appetising turned out to be surprisingly appealing. Early Tudor recipes have a certain North African flair about them – mixing a savoury meaty dish with sweet, dried fruit, and I can assure you there is something for everyone: the meat lover, the vegetarian, the sweet tooth and the salad enthusiast.

All recipes can be achieved, even by beginners, and at the end of the notes at the back of the book there is a list of contacts should you require some assistance in the making of these dishes. With the launch of the book, I will also start a video blog where you can follow me preparing these dishes.

English recipe manuscripts and cookery books in Tudor England

For this cookery book I have chosen recipes from all original recipe collections in the English language covering a period from 1485-1603. I have included the authentic recipes and 'humoral qualities' with individual ingredients listed in the recipes, where possible, allowing you to create your very own specific healthy meal based on your humoral needs.

Ideas about diet and healthy eating go right back to antiquity when food was seen as medicine that could be used to address the imbalances of the human body's individual make-up. A food's quality could be tempered with or 'corrected' by different ways of cooking, as well as the use of condiments like vinegar, spices and sugar. This was a science in itself and therefore there was a real need to bring that sort of knowledge to as many literate people as possible, which explains why cookery books were one of the very first genre of books ever to be printed.

With the beginning of the new century, the first printed cookery books in the English language started to appear in the early 1500s. *A noble Boke of Festes Ryall and Cokery*

(London: Richard Pynson, 1500) was the first *printed* cookery book in England.[5] It delivered no new recipes or concepts and was not addressed to a particular audience, but copied the menus and recipes from earlier manuscripts.

At around the same time, a small anonymous book with the title *This is the Boke of Cokery* appeared. A little later, in about 1508, a carving manual by the name of *Here Begynneth the Boke of Kervynge*, printed by Wynkyn de Worde, hit the market. This book is mostly covering the areas of how to carve various meats and how to serve food, but it also lists the right sauce for all the various meats. These listed sauces show us quite clearly that food in the final days of Henry VII's reign had changed little from medieval taste and food texture. These standard medieval sauces are very thin in texture and made from verjuice, a mild crab apple vinegar, and spices such as cinnamon, nutmeg, mace, ginger, pepper, cloves and ginger. Towards the end of his son Henry VIII's reign, we are beginning to witness change.

One of the most extensive and well-preserved collections of such early manuscripts about food with recipes is located in the library of Holkham Hall in Norfolk (see photograph on next page).

This unique collection was later published as *A Noble Boke off Cookry ffor a prynce houssolde or eny other stately houssolde* and was edited by Mrs Alexander Napier (Robina Napier) in 1882. The great jurist Sir Edward Coke possessed such a copy. The collection of recipes begins with menus for royal and other important feasts. Originally, there were 281 recipes and the title of each one written in red. Recipes are mostly for meat, poultry, fish, pottages, sauces, pies, and some vegetables, but few for fruits or other sweet dishes. The style of recipe is very different from the modern kind with no quantities or measurements given. They generally lack proper cooking instructions but sometimes give a detailed description on how to slaughter an animal, which is brutal and not for the faint-hearted. I was surprised to find no evidence of it having been used when I had the privilege to study it. The manuscript lacks food stains, which one would expect. This strongly indicates that the manuscripts were used purely for reference.

By the 1540s the market for cookery books also aimed to approach a wider, less affluent 'middling' class and in 1545 the *A Propre new booke of Cokery* was published (London: Richard Lant & Richard Banker) with later editions. This is the first cookbook of Renaissance England which is not just a copy of earlier recipes. It begins to diverge from previous centuries and displays a new emphasis on herbs, while the popular spices from medieval times are only used in moderation. The ingredients used are more widely available, and the serving sizes are relatively small. Ingredients listed can be purchased in shops rather than having to be supplied from your own large estate. The recipes range from simple pies, modest egg dishes and fritters to stewed beef or mutton dishes. The dishes are less influenced by the French taste, still popular in the early 1500s, and have no French-inspired names. The recipes are more straightforward in their description and ingredients are less exclusive. The book also contains advice on 'Best food in season' and menu suggestions.

Many of the recipes from this book were later readily copied and published in other books as there was no copyright at that time. Writers lifted whole sections or even entire works from other authors and published them under their own name. This cookery book is perhaps the first reliable source we have on what normal people really ate and was a real best-seller. The 1557 edition is thought to have been used by Archbishop of Canterbury (1559-75) Matthew

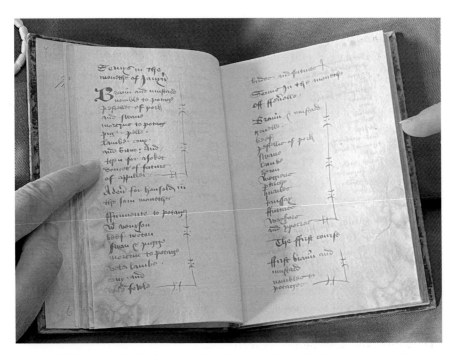

Brigitte Webster (with kind permission from the Earl of Leicester and the Trustees of the Holkham Estate)

Parker's wife, Margaret, in 1560 when Queen Elizabeth I came to Lambeth Palace to dine. This edition was transcribed and published in 1995 (Bristol Stuart Press) and edited by Jane Huggert. A facsimile, edited by Anne Ahmed, was published in 2002 (Corpus Christie College, Parker Library). The 1575 edition is held at the British Library (E 309).

Towards the end of Elizabeth's reign a number of cookbooks started to be published and the authors most freely copied from each other, which makes it rather challenging, if not impossible to determine where a particular recipe appeared first. Many of these cookery books were published anonymously and without precise publication dates. Those recipe books still contained notions of nourishment classification and medicinal recipes.

During the medieval age English cuisine had much of a French flavour, but by the end of the sixteenth century chefs and nobility were looking to Italy for fashion and culinary inspiration instead. It therefore comes as no surprise that several Italian cookery books with the catchy name of 'secrets' caught the imagination of the English who had a number of those books translated into English.

The secretes of the Reverende Maister Alexis of Piemovnt was first originally published in Venice in 1555 by the Italian physician Girolamo Ruscelli (1500-1566) under his pseudonym Alexius Pedemontanus. His work was translated into Latin, English, French, German, Spanish and Polish. The English translation appeared in November 1558, translated from the French version by Wyllyam Warde.

This book is understood to be the introduction to a new movement, the 'hunt for secrets'; a journey to unlock the secrets of nature, which also involved cookery and the process of change to ingredients due to cooking them. This was an immensely popular food reference book with twelve recipes for confitures in the third part and over a hundred later editions.

John Partridge, Elizabethan author of poetry and popular literature, cashed in on the bandwagon of a growing female market in cookery books in the sixteenth century and slightly deviated from his normal genre by publishing *The Treasurie of commodious Conceits & hidden Secrets* in 1573 through Richard Jones. Although almost nothing is known about the author himself, his cookery book started a new approach to cookery by appealing to a diverse readership as laid out in its full title: *The Treasurie of Commodious Conceits, & Hidden Secrets and may Be Called, the Huswives Closet, of Healthfull Provision. Mete and neccesarie for the profitable use of all estates both men and women.*

Although it addresses both genders, it was really aimed at the affluent lady and the womenfolk of the urban professional. Its audience was the middle-class housewife who was interested in guidance on how to create 'fake' or 'mock' food, something that appealed to the middling sort as well as those keen to adhere to a strict Lenten food diet. These food fakery dishes, which imitate the look of exclusive game birds, differ from the medieval examples in that the sixteenth-century instructions tells you how to achieve the same effect 'on a budget'.

Originals of the 1573 printing are held at the Folger Shakespeare Library and the Henry E. Huntington Library, but one can access various online versions.

Not all popular recipe books were geared towards cookery alone. *The VVidowes Treasurie* by John Partridge (1582/1588) is a cookery-cum-medicine book. Partridge used a friend's household book or recipe collection for the private use of a 'gentlewoman in the country', and in 1585 published it under his own name. It contains recipes for confectionary, preserves and other, all in the name of medicine of course. The British Library holds a copy of the 1595 edition at the British Library (Shelf mark: C.104.e.32(2)), and the 1631 edition at the Wellcome Collection can be accessed online.

Some authors preferred to remain anonymous, like 'A.W' who gathered the recipes for *A BOOKE of Cookery very necessary* which was printed in London

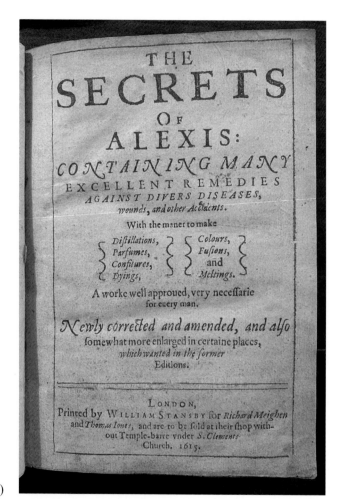

Brigitte Webster
(author's own copy)

by John Allde, first in 1584 and then again in 1591 by Edward Allde. This cookery book includes recipes neatly arranged into chapters: sauces, stewed and boiled, baked, roasted meat and fish as well as tarts. Several recipes are identical to *A Proper New Book of Cookrey*, but in Tudor England that posed no problem and perhaps was even seen as a kind of endorsement. You can access this cookery book online: the 1587 version is available through the University of Leeds.

Between 1580 and 1600 there was a real flurry of editions of very small books containing mainly culinary recipes, some specifically addressed to women. Their titles suggested that they contained valuable knowledge, such as Thomas Dawson's *The good husvvifes Ievvell*, printed in London and sold by Edward White in 1596. This book harks back to medieval basics, tying them in with new ideas and ingredients. It is also the first cookery book to mention sweet potatoes. Strange to us today, the recipes are presented without any form of organisation. You can check it out at the British Library (Shelf mark C.104.e.32(3)), the Bodleian and one in the Huntington (E213) gallery. Or if you prefer, find a copy online. A copy of the 1596 edition can be found at the British Library (E 197). It is often bound with the second part from a year later: *The Second part of the good hus-wiues Iewell*. As so often, little is known about Thomas Dawson, the author.

Another anonymous cookery book hit the market in 1588 with the most promising title of *The Good Hous-wiues Treasurie* – its full title being *The Good Hous-wiues Treasurie. Beeing a verye necessarie Booke instructing to the dressing of Meates, Hereunto is also annexed, sundrie holsome Medicines for diuers diseases*. This book can be viewed at the British Library (E 548) or accessed online.

One of my personal favourite cookery books of that time is *The good Huswifes Handmaide for the Kitchin*, first published in 1588. What makes this one significant is that it is the one of the first to address the woman who is doing the cookery or managing the household. Clearly this book is aimed at the affluent lady of the house who could also afford to purchase a book, and as many recipes call for game, one of the most prestigious meats, presumably the audience was located at a country estate. The proportions suggest a moderate-sized family. Many of the dishes are simply boiled or stewed, but it is clear that this book was aimed at a household with a bread oven. Spices are used but nowhere as much in quantity as the century before. There is a striking similarity between this edition and Thomas Dawson's *Book of Cookerie* (1585/97) which makes some believe that he is also the author of this book. The transcript, edited by Stuart Peachey (1992), can be purchased from Stuart Press, 24 Sandford Road, Bristol, or access the book online. An imperfect copy is held at the Bodleian Library (E 176, E 875).

The most exciting recipes, in my opinion, are to be found in *Epulario or The Italian Banquet* which was translated into English from Italian in 1598. It was first published in Venice in 1516. The recipes really do differ from the English cookery books and have a refreshing Italian twist to them. There are copies held at the Bodleian, Huntington (E 539), and University of Chicago, or accessed online.

The last popular cookery book that came out before the end of the Tudor era was *Delightes for Ladies* by Sir Hugh Plat, who published the first edition in 1602 through Peter Short in London. Hugh Plat(t) (1552-1608/11) was an unlikely candidate for writing a cookery book. As a lawyer he spent most of his time writing about agriculture and gardening, but clearly must have had a passion for food to produce such a best-seller without any professional background in this field. A copy of this book is held at the British Library (E1733).

The sixteenth century fired up a passion for cookery and sparked off a new food-related debate which was only made possible by the discovery of the printing press a century earlier. The focus on the male audience in the beginning changed entirely to the focus of the lady of the house by the close of the century. Sadly, it would take another half a century for the first female cookery book author to come forward.

Chapter 1

SPRING

Food in Spring

The early spring was probably the most challenging time for people at the lower end of Tudor society with food stocks running low and nature not yet providing edibles to forage and barely enough fresh cultivated greenery to feed a family.

This was the season of extremes: weather, food supply and diets: from frosty temperatures in March to balmy sunshine in May; from rock-hard stockfish in Lent to fresh, juicy meat at Easter; from abstinence to gluttony; from fast to feast; from dried beans and peas to fresh salad leaves – this season had it all.

In 1584 Physician Thomas Cogan reminds us that even seasons had humors ascribed to them. He states that 'spring time beginneth in March when the Sunne entereth into Aries, and is in temperature, not hot and moyst after the old opinion but in a meane without all excesse, as Galen proveth, and the equall mixture of the foure qualities in it'. He further states that spring is the healthiest season, despite the fact that the beginning might bring winter and the end summery conditions. This radical change obviously requires a very different approach to what should be eaten. He confirms that in March the 'dyet should bee according to Winter', and 'in the latter part of the Spring, wherein wee should eate but a little meate much like as in Summer, yet not so much as in Winter, nor so little as in Summer'. His entry on his publication of *The Haven of Health* finishes with some good sensible advice: Whatever you eat make sure it is of good nourishment – a Tudor way to express a balanced and healthy diet.[1] Sir Thomas Elyot, a physician in Henry VIII's time, puts spring between the eighth of February and the eighth of May.[2]

Fast Days and Lent

Collop Monday and Shrove Tuesday mark the end of Carnival (Latin *Carne vale* = goodbye to meat) and with Ash Wednesday signals the beginning of

Lent, a period of forty days without meat, dairy or eggs; a time of penitence and abstinence from gluttony and consumption of luxury food.

In medieval times and through Henry VIII's reign, people were expected to abstain from meat on religious grounds and eat fish instead, not only on Fridays and Saturdays but also throughout Lent and on the eves of some Saint's days, which was almost half the days of the year.

No meat was allowed on Fridays to commemorate the crucifixion and the food intake was reduced to one meal a day. Saturdays were meat-free in respect of the Virgin Mary.

Ember Days, which marked the four quarters of the year, were meat-free but dairy products were allowed. The really long periods of fasting with no animal products were Lent (Ash Wednesday to Easter) and Advent (First Sunday in the four weeks before Christmas until Christmas Day). Meat days were also known as 'fat' days and fish days as 'lean' days. Lean days also meant fewer meals (only midday dinner).

Just like with meat, the ability to offer high-status fish to guests reflected one's social standing. Fish, like other foods, was invested with symbolic meaning and Lent could be an opportunity for consuming high-value fish (bream, carp, salmon, trout) that distinguished the foodways of the well-to-do from those of labourers who were left to eat the lowest quality – salted fish and rock-hard stockfish.

The Flemish artist Pieter Bruegel the Elder often used food as a way to satirise political and social issues. His works, and those of his followers, illustrate the ways that cultural representations both reflected and influenced what people ate. In the painting *The fight between carnival and Lent*, 1559, he uses the seasonal food fight to represent the religious conflicts that divided people in sixteenth-century England and Europe. Carnival's atmosphere of the world turned upside down had made it a time of social and political protest.

Under Edward VI religious fish days were cancelled as a protest against the Roman Catholic symbols of Popery. The instrumental player of the Protestant movement, the Swiss Huldrych Zwingli, famously defied the rules of Lenten abstinence from meat by cooking and eating sausages on Ash Wednesday in 1522. Martin Luther preached in the same year that people were free to eat any kind of food. He did, though, admit that he himself also found it hard to eat meat on Fridays and during Lent.

In England, however, by 1548 fish days had to be reintroduced – not for religious, but for economic and political reasons and included both Fridays and Saturdays. One of the reasons was that the price of meat started to rise sharply and many poor people could no longer afford any.

In a statute of 1563, it was stressed that every Wednesday and Saturday had to be a fish day unless they fell in the week of Easter or Christmas. This helped to keep up the numbers of cattle stock but also promoted fisheries, shipbuilding and the training of mariners. Breaking these rules would result in a fine or time in prison. The chronically ill were exempt. The selling of meat on those days was not permitted and was also punishable.

In 1587, in his contemporary account of Tudor social life, William Harrison confirms that the English were free to eat what they liked and when they liked – apart from the days when meat was forbidden:

> there is no restraint of any meat, either for religion's sake or public order, in England, but it is lawful for every man to feed upon whatsoever he is able to purchase, except it be upon those days whereon eating of flesh is especially forbidden by the laws of the realm, which order is taken only to the end our numbers of cattle may be the better increased and that abundance of fish which the sea yieldth more generally received.

By 1585 Wednesday restrictions were lifted, but in a further act of 1593 it is made clear that eating meat on a fish day was not tolerated and offenders disobeying this regulation were fined or put in prison. Those turning a blind eye on offenders risked getting fined themselves and the head of a house was legally responsible for all the people within his household.

Indeed, at court and other establishments this rule was regularly broken and meat was served on Wednesdays. Of course, you could buy a licence freeing you from all these dietary restrictions and many wealthy families showed no drop in their consumption of meat throughout the forty days of Lent.

For most people, their Lenten diet of grains, vegetables and legumes was not too different from what they might have eaten on most days outside Lent. The broad bean, or fava bean, was largely regarded as a staple for the poor, in particular throughout Lent. Easily dried, it kept for months and was used in pottages or could be turned into some kind of mash.

The affluent class was financially able to import permitted dairy alternatives such as olive oil for suet or lard, almonds for making a milk substitute, and dried fruit such as figs and dates. For the people at the bottom of the social ladder there was just abstinence.

Meat- and dairy-free food restrictions during Lent were designed for Italy's warmer climate with olive trees and almond trees. It did not take into account the fact that the climate in Northern Europe did not allow for these plants to grow and so their produce had to be imported at great cost and out of the reach of the poor. It is one reason why in the late 1400s several countries were exempt from abstinence from butter. In countries without this exemption, people with money – Erasmus being one of them – could purchase a dispensation from the church. Towards the end of the sixteenth century we see increasing evidence of people finding ways around dietary abstinence and self-denial of luxurious food, clearly endorsed by contemporary cookery books giving lots of advice on how to make fish in special ways, and the use of high-status, expensive and exotic ingredients such as sugar and imported food like olive oil, figs, dates and sugar.

Unlike feasting, little material culture remains of this strict fasting regime.

Overeating was condemned but so too was excessive abstinence which was considered harmful. We gain a true insight into contemporary Lenten food through authors like Thomas Tusser with this entry on *Marches husbandrrie* (1577 and 1580):

> Now leekes are in season, for pottage full good.
> And spareth the milchcow and purgeth the blood.
> These hauing, with peason for pottage in Lent,
> Thou sparest both otemell and bread to be spent.

Shrove Tuesday and Easter

Collop Monday was the day to clear the larder of meat and bacon and Shrove Tuesday to use up eggs and dairy, resulting in pancakes, fritters or waffles.

As the seasons turned, fasting flowed back into feasting and after the punishing forty days of Lent, Easter was the great release. The events of Christ's life in the week leading up to Easter found their echo in pre-reformation food customs.

Easter has always been associated particularly with eggs and lamb, but there are other foods that play a part in the days of Eastertide. Maundy Thursday is the occasion of the Last Supper and was marked by almsgiving and often special foods for the poor such as barley bread, given in 'maunds', or baskets. Interestingly, many Christian paintings and illuminations show the Last Supper with fish – yet it is far more likely that not fish but lamb, a typical Passover dish, was shared that evening.

In medieval times, it became customary for the sovereign to provide a meal and also to present gifts of clothing, food and money to the poor. In 1556 the secretary to Cardinal Pole witnessed Mary I washing feet on Maundy Thursday and afterwards offering salted fish and large loaves of bread to the poor.

Good Friday derived from the German *Gottes Freitag* ('God's Friday'). This was the day in the year on which most people did try to fast – except for bread and drink.

The still popular hot cross buns, spiced sweet buns made with currants or raisins and marked with a cross on top, may be as old as ancient Greek but there is also another theory, that they originate from St Albans in Hertfordshire, where brother Thomas Rocliffe, a fourteenth-century monk at St Albans Abbey, developed a recipe for 'Alban Bun' and distributed these buns to the local poor on Good Friday starting in 1361. The original recipe of the Alban bun claims to be the forerunner of the modern hot cross bun, but the cross is cut into the top of the bun before being baked rather than piped on top.

Easter Sunday put meat, diary, eggs and cheese back on the menu. However, none of it was meant to be eaten before the first Mass that day, though the rector of a village near Lincoln knew how to lure the hungry folk into his church – by serving eggs and bacon!

For the nobility, lamb, the symbol of the resurrection of Christ being named the 'Lamb of God', featured on the tables of Easter Sunday as Easter also falls during the lambing season. Lamb used to be a typical Passover food and so was most likely the food that was served at the Last Supper, however, in Christian medieval prayer books, the lamb was replaced with fish to be in line with the Lenten diet.

Throughout Lent, many eggs that were laid were hard boiled to help preserve them for later. The hiding of the eggs by the parents for children to find, is believed to be a way of representing the disciples finding the risen Christ in the tomb on Easter Sunday. It is said that this tradition might have been started by Martin Luther when he and other men were hiding the eggs for women and children to find. In the countryside, peasants brought eggs to their lords, a typical customary rent in kind, and the lord frequently reciprocated with a feast for his servants on Easter Sunday.

The well-known Simnel cake was originally made for the middle Sunday of Lent, when the forty-day fast would be relaxed. This was known as Laetare Sunday, Mothering Sunday, and Simnel Sunday. This was the day when the congregations of the daughter churches of the parish went to the mother church (abbey). Simnel cakes have been baked since the Middle Ages and it is believed that the word comes from the Latin *simila* (very fine flour made from wheat – which also gives us the word semolina). This cake was difficult to make and the baking of a Simnel cake for Mothering Sunday was also a girl's test of her baking skills. This cake would not be eaten until Easter Sunday.

Fish

Fishponds, once the privilege of monasteries and manors only, were increasing in numbers near lesser estates and farmhouses by the beginning of the sixteenth century. There are numerous estate accounts which provide us with very detailed information on how much fish and what type was provided to the landed gentry throughout Lent from ponds and moats.

In his book *Plenti and Grase* Mark Dawson gives many examples of freshwater fish such as bream, pickerel (small pike), tench, barbel, perch and grayling (ling) used from fishponds at the Willoughbys' estates of Wollaton and Middleton Hall. Carp, a long-established fish on the Continent, only found favour in England during the Tudor age. To obtain fish from rivers you had to have a licence. Freshwater fish, according to William Harrison, was sold by the inch, measured from the eye to the tail.

Most fresh fish, both, freshwater and sea, was purchased locally and was caught in the North Sea or came from fishponds. Fresh maritime fish was mostly purchased for the colder months and comprised turbot, cod, thornback, skate, haddock and plaice, as well as oysters, cockles, mussels and crabs.

The most common freshwater fish, eel, came from the fens in East Anglia and features in many recipes. Roach and tench were a common sight on the dining table, bream and pike were considered luxuries in 1500.

Those with deep pockets had a wide variety of fresh fish available. Henry VIII selected nineteen meat-free dishes for his first course at dinner with a further fifteen for his second, as we learn from Peter Brears in his book *Cooking & Dining in Tudor and Early Stuart England*. Amongst the choice fish featured were porpoise, salmon, sturgeon, halibut, lampreys, crabs, lobsters and shrimps. His servants would have been offered ling, cod, plaice and whiting instead.

Fresh fish was also a popular gift, especially high-status fish such as salmon, pike, sturgeon and bream, and generally remained a luxury food of choice for the wealthy.

As the demand for fish was not met by freshwater fish only, deep-sea fishing started to expand. Fish for Lent was caught in June the year before, salted, dried or cured and sold in the autumn at fairs for supply through the winter and Lent the next year.

Salt fish was eaten all through the year but in greater numbers during Lent.

Large stocks of cod around Iceland were caught and salted on board ships by the English, Scottish and Scandinavian fisheries and sold as salt fish, ling being top quality and haberden the cheaper option. Thomas Tusser, in his 1580 edition of the *Fiue hundred pointes of good Husbandrie*, gives sound advice on making the fish last and prevent it from going off.

Both saltfish and lingfish (if any ye haue)
Through shifting and drieng from rotting go saue:
Least winter with moistnes doo make it relent,
And put it in hazard before it be spent.

Broome fagot is best to drie haberden on,
Lay boord vpon ladder if fagots be on.
For breaking (in turning) haue verie good eie,
And blame not the wind, so the weather be drie.

Salted and dried hake was known as 'Poor John' and 'Lobbe' was salted pollack.

Another cheap salt fish was green-fish, which was uncured, not dried salted fish – usually cod – and packed into barrels. Green fish kept less well than the dried salted fish. Headless cod, stored in barrels, was found on the *Mary Rose*.

In 1599 Thomas Nash claims that Great Yarmouth in Norfolk produced the best cured fish, and physician Andrew Boorde also confirmed that the English were leaders in producing the best salt fish: 'Of all nacyons and countres, England is beste seruyd of Fysshe, not onley of al maner of see-fysshe, but also of fresshe- water fysshe, and all maner of sortes of salte-fysshe.'

Stockfish is basic, air-dried, unsalted cod and was predominately produced and sourced from Scandinavia. It was the cheapest form of preserved fish and lasted for months but required many days of pre-soaking before it could be used for cooking, and, on occasion, also the use of a mallet to break it into pieces. It is this preserved fish that declined in sixteenth-century England.

Maritime fish was generally purchased from a number of markets that specialised in bulk purchase such as Stourbridge, near Cambridge. Stourbridge was the biggest fair and was held in September. People travelled to it from all over the country and abroad. Accounts from Bess of Hardwick, John Willoughby of Wollaton Hall in Nottingham and the Shuttleworth family, all made regular trips there to stock up on fish and at Lichfield Fair.

Perhaps rather strange to us, any animal that was observed living in or near the water counted as suitable food for 'fish days': this included beavers and various seabirds.

Meat from Young Animals

To the Tudors, next to bread, meat was the most important foodstuff because animal flesh was considered the closest in substance and essence to the human body. Any food consumed was rated by how quickly and easily it was converted into human body substance. In a time when health-conscious upper-class members of society were advised to eat meat to suit their complexion (their physical make-up), it was necessary to know the humors of individual meat.

The English proverb 'Yong flesh and old fish doth men best feed' confirms that even in the sixteenth century people preferred the taste of succulent, young animals over mature ones.[3] However, the meat of weaned young animals which was 'less clammy and more wholesom' was better regarded.

William Harrison (1535-93) claims that in England, veal and lamb are taken for 'necessary dishes at every feast amongst the commonality'.[4] Late-sixteenth-century cookery books in England show a preference for mutton and lamb over beef, veal and pork – a theory much supported by Thomas Cogan (1584) claiming that mutton (lamb) was eaten more than any other. However, this might just have been a trend starting around 1550.

Lamb

An Elizabethan cookery book advises that lamb is best between Christmas and Lent and good from Easter to Whitsuntide. Suckling lamb was considered too 'moist' in humors to be healthy, but a year-old lamb was deemed one of the best meats of choice. In 1584 Thomas Cogan states that lamb is not recommended for aged men and, contrary to veal, should be eaten rather under-roasted than over.[5] Members of the Drapers' Company in London enjoyed a whole lamb as part of their annual company dinner in 1564-65.[6]

Veal

Veal is also associated with Easter, according to Thomas Tusser's *Hundred Points of Good Husbandry* (1557): 'When Easter come who knows not than/ That veal and bacon is the man/ And Martilmas beef doth bear good tack/When country folks do dainties lack'.

The Elizabethan cookery book *The good Huswifes Handmaide for the Kitchin* (1594), however, claims that veal is good all year round but best in January and February.

In 1547 physician Andrew Boorde had claimed in his book *A Dyetary of Helth* (1542) that veal was the best meat of all.[7] A little later, Thomas Muffet (1553-1604) only partially agrees but insists that in the English climate the fairly cold and moist humors of veal must be corrected by dry roasting the meat or it will be 'unwholsom', which would have been bad news for health-minded people. Muffet also draws attention to the benefit of a slightly older calf of at least a month in age as the nourishment is sounder and more wholesome. He further finds the need to remind us that a male calf tastes sweeter and better.[8] In 1599 priest and academic Henry Butts advises in his *Dyets dry dinner* that veal is temperate in all qualities and good for all seasons, ages and constitutions. The flesh is 'holesome' for all that exercise much but naturally 'hurteth the weake or those in recouery'.[9]

Suckling pig

Thomas Cogan says that young pigs are generally called 'roasting pigges' and commonly eaten. The meat accounts as light, despite not being very wholesome due to excess moisture and sliminess, which luckily can be easily corrected with some good wine.[10]

Kid

There are very few English recipes from the Tudor period that use kid or goat. William Harrison, however, does mention both in his *The Description of England* from 1587, and states that there are plenty of goats in the west parts of England and that the 'bodies of their young kids are judged very profitable and therefore inquired for of many far and near'.[11] Thomas Muffet, an English physician, tells us that red and black kids taste better than white ones and the best flesh comes from kids above a fortnight old as it is more wholesome and nourishing. He further explains that the flesh is quickly digested and is temperately hot and moist under the age of six weeks old.'[12]

Gosling

In 1599 Butts states that gosling flesh is hot in the first and moist in the second degree making them suitable for people who are physically active and have a 'hot' stomach in cold countries like England. To balance the humors, roasting and the use of spices are recommended. *The good Huswifes Handmaide for the Kitchin* from the 1594 edition, states, that 'young green geese' were the best.[13]

In April 1530, a reward of 4s 8d was paid by the Privy Purse of Henry VIII for the delivery of '*grene gees*' (under four months old), strongly indicating that young geese were also on the menu at Henry's court.[14] The Willoughby household at Wollaton Hall consumed seventeen goslings in 1588 and between 1598-99 it was thirteen.[15] *The Dinner Book of the London Draper's Company* shows several entries for green geese and goose.[16]

White meats

In Tudor times, dairy goods, also known by the derogatory name of 'white meats', had a fairly low status in the food hierarchy in general and were regarded as pre-eminently poor men's food. As the physician Thomas Cogan explains, 'because they are not plainely flesh, they are permitted to be eaten upon the fish dayes', but they were off the menu during the much stricter diet in Lent and Advent.

Early in the Tudor period, dairy food was ignored on the political scene and dairy women sold their produce only in local markets. Male cheesemongers, however, were in charge in London. Cheese was an everyday food for working men, especially convenient in the field. In grand houses cheese was tolerated and needed to feed the staff above labouring rank. Towards the end of the sixteenth century, we clearly see a change in the attitude towards cheese and its arrival at the dining table of the affluent. William Harrison's observations indicate this change of perceptions regarding dairy. According to him, dairy produce was 'never so dear' in his days.[17]

The rising demand for cheeses had also made them more expensive. There was a considerable difference in price between soft and hard cheese. Soft cheese was quickly prepared and cheap to make in contrast to the long-maturing and therefore costly hard cheese that the affluent class consumed. This stands in complete contrast to the universal agreement amongst physicians that the harder, drier and more aged the cheese was, the more difficult it was to digest and the less suited it was to anyone but the labourer.

Andrew Boorde identified the four sorts of cheese: hard, soft, green (i.e., fresh) and spermyse, which was infused with the juices of herbs and can still be purchased as 'Derby Sage'. Fresh (green) cheese he labels 'cold and moyste', soft cheese is hot and moist, hard cheese hot and dry, and he explains that the 'nature' of spermyse depends on the herbs being used.

The rich quickly developed a taste for fancy foreign cheese. Cheese from France (Angelot) Italy (Parmesan) and Holland were particularly popular and a desired gift.

A few English cheeses also made it to the top. Cheshire cheese was by far the most respected one, followed by Shropshire cheese. Cheshire cheese was acclaimed by John Speed as the best in Europe. Banbury cheese is first recorded by name in 1430. It was sold traditionally at a cheese fair on the first Thursday after Old Michaelmas in Banbury. It was made from cow's milk, golden yellow in colour with a strong flavour. Its thin shape surrounded by an outer skin is the reason for an insult used by William Shakespeare in *The Merry Wives of Windsor* when Bardolph addresses Abraham Slender with 'You Banbury cheese'! (1597, 1.1.126). Sadly, the cheese is no longer produced, but there is an original fifteenth-/sixteenth-century recipe at the British Library (Sloane MS1201).

Suffolk and Essex cheese were probably made from skimmed milk which made them cheaper, and they often feature in the household accounts of the

Petre family at Ingatestone Hall in Essex where they were used for the servants. Suffolk and Essex cheeses were often described as hard and dry, which makes their presentation to the court by Lady Elizabeth Oxford of the De Vere family from Castle Hedingham in Essex quite a mystery.[18] One can only assume, that those were made under her strict supervision as the bearer was rewarded with a healthy 18s and 8d. Tudor poet John Skelton (1460-1529) draws a crude picture for cheese from Essex:

> A cantle of Essex cheese
> Was well a foot thick
> Full of maggots quick:
> It was huge and great
> And mighty strong meat
> For the devil to eat,
> It was tart and pungete.

English recipes generally do not list cheese as a cooking ingredient (except for tart of cheese), but Welsh cheese was toasted if we are to believe Andrew Boorde's account from 1540. Cheese was often served at the close of a meal as it was regarded as an efficient 'seal' for the cooking process that took place inside the stomach. Physician Edmund Hollings (1556-1612) observes that a small quantity of cheese constitutes a big meal because it is filling and nutritious.[19]

Thomas Muffet (1553-1604) shares with his readers what he considers a good, wholesome cheese: 'neither too soft nor too hard, too close, nor yet spongy, too clammy, nor yet crumbling, too salty, nor yet unsavoury, too dry, nor yet weeping, pleasantly, not strongly smelling, easily melting in the mouth and never burning as it is toasted at the fire.' He also mentions several cheeses by name: Essex, Parmesan, Angelot, Cheshire and Banbury. In his opinion, they can be compared to the quality of cheeses from Holland.[20]

Imported cheese was quite expensive as taxes had to be paid, clearly shown in the Norwich Accounts for the Customs on Strangers' Goods and merchandise of the Great Yarmouth Assembly minutes of June 1585: Peter Peterson, alien, was charged import tax on 'cheeze ratyd at 30s'. There are also several entries on 'Hollond Cheese'.[21]

The cheese's ability to keep made it also ideal for army daily rations and most armies of that time would allow one pound of cheese, as Ken Albala explains in his book *A cultural history of food in the Renaissance*.[22]

It appears that the nobility purchased large amounts of cheese not for themselves but mostly for their servants and workforce. Cheese also features in sixteenth-century wills. On 7 November 1577 John Cartmell, gentleman of Wisdens in the parish of Hornchurch, left his best cheese to Audrey his wife in his will.[23]

The accounts of wealthy households show that cheese was also a welcome gift. The account of William Chancy 1558-9 for Robert Dudley, Earl of Leicester, show an entry for cheese: Mr Bridges was rewarded 3s 4d for bringing 'cheasis & bakemeats'.[24] On 13 August 1537 John Worth sent Cromwell 'a dozen of Picardy cheeses which, I am informed, you like',[25] and in a letter to Lord Lisle dated 20 July 1533, Sir William Kingston thanks him for the good cheese that he had received.[26]

Cheese was even gifted to the king. In June 1530 the bearers of cheese for the king were rewarded 20s.[27] Cheese also worked as a bribe. The Expenses records of the Judges of Assize Riding the Western and Oxford circuits show that cheese gifts were received from Mr Evans in 1601.[28]

In Tudor England, butter was not as much made or eaten by ordinary folk as pork lard and beef suet which were cheaper and more plentiful. The custom of eating butter on bread was most likely introduced by Flemish and Dutch settlers in Elizabethan England. In 1567 one Flemish settler in Norwich wrote to his wife in Ypres telling her how his fellow countrymen were making their own butter, 'for here it is all pig's fat'.[29]

In 1587 William Harrison noted that butter was served as a starter on fish days, very much like the 'Belgies' were accustomed.[30] Thomas Cogan considers fresh butter very wholesome, especially if eaten in the morning. He reminds his readers of the old English proverb: 'Butter is Gold in the morning, And Silver at noone, And lead at night'.[31] Thomas Muffet explains that butter is 'cream twice laboured', based on the belief that milk is 'nothing but blood twise'.[32] Henry Butts adds in 1599 that butter is hot and moist in the beginning of the second degree and is better suited for the elderly than the young.

The Flemish also imported butter from their home country to England, as can be seen by numerous records showing the import duty paid on such goods. Pascher Hubert, Alien, was charged 2s on 30 June 1585 for the custom of six barrels of butter rated by Mr Mayor at 12s 1d and Peter Peters had to pay 12d on 24 July for three 'barrelles of butter ratyd at vi/I'.[33]

Perhaps rather odd to us is the occasional appearance of butter in sixteenth-century wills. The will of Braintree (Essex) yeoman Richard Man, dated 27 October 1571, mentions 'a firkin of butter' to be given to his wife, Joan.[34]

Milk was believed to be 'twice-concocted blood' and most people only drank milk occasionally as an ingredient in possets, a mixture with wine, milk and sugar. Milk was cold and moist in its properties and could be corrected with hot and dry honey or salt. Cogan feels that it is best drunk in the morning with spearmint, a little sugar and pure honey.[35] Milk does not often appear in household accounts but 16s 8d was spent on fourteen gallons of cream and one gallon of milk between 1566 and 67 by the London Drapers' Company at their annual feast.[36]

Cream does not feature a lot in recipes during the early years of the Tudor reign. It was considered hot and moist in its humoral make-up and sugar or honey was considered the most suitable 'corrective' as advised in 1599 by Henry Butts. Thomas Cogan calls cream 'the very head or heart of Milke' and explains that 'clouted Creame' is made by setting the milk over a small fire until the cream starts to thicken.

Cream was mostly used for making butter but during the sixteenth century a new way of using cream was celebrated by the affluent, 'snow', which is cream and whipped egg white (see recipe in chapter four). Cream was an occasional treat for the wealthy in form of strawberries and cream. Andrew Boorde referred to it as a rural man's banquet and in his opinion, cream is eaten more for a sensual appetite than for any health benefits and 'such bankettes hath put men in ieoperdy of theyr lyues'.

In the final years of the sixteenth century we see cream being used by the well-to-do in various culinary applications and food for a banquet. Thomas Moffett mentions 'custards' and explains that they are 'less offensive to the stomach, and of better nourishment', because the cream has been boiled. However, he does criticise the habit of eating cream at the end of a meal, when it would be much better to do so at the beginning. Cream features twice in *The Dinner Book of the London Drapers' Company* – for the feast dinner on the first Monday in August 1564, 14s 4d was spent on cream and for the consumption of cream at the 1567 event 16s 8d was paid for fourteen gallons of cream and one gallon of milk.[37] John Lane, the person in charge of Thetford Priory's dairy, records the sum of 4s 8d for fourteen gallons of 'creem' on 22 October 1515.[38]

Eggs were among the most prevalent foods at all levels of society. Regarded as very nourishing, they were also valued as healthy food and easily digested. Most physicians recommended poached egg, but recipes show that they were also fried, boiled, scrambled, roasted and even cooked on a spit! Eggs were also used to thicken pottages and sauces, and for the first time used in pastry dough which made pies and pastie crusts edible. Eggs also provided the perfect nourishment for people of all ages, complexions and in all seasons, and were suitable even on fish days, except for Lent and Advent. The Tudors definitely preferred the yolk, which was considered 'temporatly hot' by Andrew Boorde who dismissed the egg white as 'viscus & colde'. He recommends poached egg at night and fresh, roasted eggs in the morning. To make them a bit more nutritious, he advises adding salt or sugar.

As a great number of eggs were needed for any feast, household accounts provide a clear understanding about the number and frequency needed for special events. The Dinner Book of the London Draper's Company shows 8d paid for eggs used for the first Quarter Dinner on the fifteenth day of November 1569.[39]

Caroline Angus, in her book *My Hearty Commendations* – transcribed letters of Thomas Cromwell – shows an entry of 4s 8d paid to Thomas Rotherham for apples and eggs on 23 December 1538 – clearly for making apple pies with edible crust for Christmas![40]

Recipes

TO MAKE PANCAKES

Transcribed original recipe

> Take new thicke Creame a pinte, foure or five yolks of Egs, a good handful of flower, and two or three spoonfuls of ale, strain them together into a faire platter, and season it with good handful of Sugar, a spoonful of Synamon, and a little Ginger: then take a frying pan, and put in a little peece pf Butter, as big as your thombe, and when it is molten browne, cast it out of your pan, and with a ladle put to the further side of your pan some of your stuffe, and hold your pan aslope, so that your stuffe may run abroad ouer all the pan, as thin as may be: then set it to the fyre, and let the fyre be verie soft, and when the one side is baked, then turne the other, and bake them as dry as ye can without burning.

The Good Huswifes Handmaide for the Kitchin, 1594 edition

Modernised recipe

- 240ml cream
- 2 egg yolks
- 2 tbsp ale

- ◆ 50g flour
- ◆ 30g sugar
- ◆ ¼ tsp ginger
- ◆ 1 tsp cinnamon
- ◆ Butter for frying

Put a little butter in your frying pan and let it melt. Mix all ingredients together in a bowl and then make your pancakes by pouring the mixture into the frying pan with a ladle, frying each one at medium heat until the first side turns golden brown. This mixture is really hard to turn over without breaking. It will help to add more flour to the mixture but by doing so, the texture will no longer be as 'very soft' as described in the original recipe above.

The measurement for flour is given as a 'handful'. Naturally it is safe to assume that Thomas Dawson's hand was larger than mine and so I felt it justified to add another 20g to the flour quantity.

These pancakes are a little tricky to fry but they are delicious!

Additional information

This is the only recipe for plain pancakes to be found in English cookery books in the Tudor era. Various spellings range from *panecake, ponkake, pannecake,* to *pankake*.

The three days of Shrovetide marked the end of the seasonal celebrations which had begun with the Twelve Days of Christmas and climaxed with Shrove Tuesday. In 1571 William Kethe, a Protestant bible translator, referred to Shrovetide as a time of 'great gluttony, surfeiting and drunkenness.' In 1586 the poet William Warner is effectively the first who makes a reference to the Shrove Tuesday pancake as 'Fast-eve pan-puffs' in his poem 'Albion's England'.[41]

This particular 'Holi-day' was a riotous orgy of indulgence during which any remaining meat and animal products, like butter and cheese, had to be consumed prior to the forty-days fast of Lent.

During the Reformation, an increasing number of people abolished practices like fasting and the aforementioned Roman Catholic feasts. Shrovetide or 'Carnival' was one of those that was the first to disappear and by the seventeenth century it was no longer celebrated in England. However, today, most Christians still eat pancakes on Shrove Tuesday, a remnant of this earlier tradition.

TO MAKE FRITTERS OF CHEESE, EGGES AND ELDER FLOWERS

Transcribed original recipe

> To make Fritters of Cheese, Egges, and Elder flowers. Take new and a little old Cheese and stampe them well, putting to it a little fine flower, and White of Egges according to the quantity you

will make, with a little Milke and good store of Sugar, stamp them all together, then take it out of the morter, and put Elder flowers as your discretion serueth. Neither beaten nor stamped. This composition would not bee too soft nor liquid, that it may bee wrought with the hand in any forme you will, then frie them in good Suet, butter, or Oyle, and send them whote to the Table.

'Epulario' (The Banquet), 1598, from the *Fourth Booke: Shewing how to dresse all kind of Fish*

Modernised recipe

- approx. 5 cleaned elderflowers
- approx. 100g ricotta cheese
- approx. 100g hard cheese (I used Cheshire cheese) – grated
- approx. 100g sugar
- approx. 100g flour
- approx. 50ml milk
- 1-2 egg whites
- Butter, oil or fat for frying

Mix all ingredients together to form a thick paste. Form little 'burgers' and fry in hot butter, oil or fat on both sides until golden brown. It is recommended to fry them slowly to make sure that all elderflowers get 'cooked' properly because they should not be consumed raw as this may lead to vomiting or diarrhoea.

Additional information

Elderflowers and berries were considered 'hot' and 'dry' in their humoral make-up.

John Gerard (1597) recommended elder leaves, boiled in a pottage, as a gentle way to purge the system. However, there is nothing gentle about the consumption of any raw part unless you consider violent vomiting or diarrhoea 'gentle'. The dried elder flowers steeped in vinegar, he praises for their wholesomeness for the stomach, and mentions that they are being used with meat to 'stirreth vp an appeitite'.[42]

PAX CAKES (PEACE BISCUITS), TRADITIONAL

Modernised recipe

To make the batter, beat one egg. Then add and beat the following until smooth: 1 cup of buttermilk, 2 tablespoon olive oil, ½ cup whole wheat flour, ¼ cup wheat germ, ¼ cup white flour, 1 tablespoon sugar, 1 tsp baking powder, ½ soda, ½ tsp salt.

Grease heated skillet or griddle pan. Pour the batter onto the hot griddle in 3-5cm diameter drops. Turn the pax cakes when bubbles show. Heat on the second side until brown.

Sprinkle with icing sugar. Cinnamon may be added if desired.

(from *The Tudor Kitchen* by Terry Breverton, 2015)

Additional information

An almost forgotten tradition associated with Palm Sunday is the giving of pax cakes. Dating back to at least 1570, these small biscuits were handed out by vicars to their congregation on Palm Sunday. The cakes carried an impress of a lamb and a flag and were originally buns. The origins of the pax cakes

ceremony lie with the family of Thomas More, vicar of Sellack and Kings Caple in 1442. He died on Palm Sunday 1448, leaving a massive £20 to a local charity.[43] According to social historian Ronald Hutton, on Palm Sunday, flowers and cakes were thrown to the congregation at the south door of the church.[44]

A TANSEY (Cake)

Transcribed original recipe

> To make Tansey. Take a little Tansey, Feverfew, Parsley and Violets, and stampe them all together and straine them with the

yolkes of eight or tenne Egges, and three or foure whites, + some Vergious, and put thereto Sugar and salt, and frie it.

The Good Huswifes Handmaide for the Kitchin, 1594 edition

Modernised recipe

- ♦ Handful of green kitchen herbs such as parsley, basil, mint, violet leaves etc, all finely chopped
- ♦ One egg yolk per person and half as many additional egg whites, beaten
- ♦ Mild apple vinegar (= 'vergious')
- ♦ Sugar & salt to taste

Mix all ingredients and fry in a greased pan on both sides.

Avoid herbs such as tansy as it can cause severe digestive problems in some people.

Additional information

The very symbol of Easter then and now, eggs also symbolized rebirth and they were a popular gift for commoners to give to their lords, hoping in return to be invited for a feast at the manor, as was the tradition. In England, this was a green-coloured omelette, sometimes also known as *Erbolat*, and was a popular choice for Easter.

Tansey was flavoured with the juices of the perennial yellow flowered herb *Tanacetum vulgare* or tansy. The young leaves of the herb tansy develop toxins with the increasing warmth and sunshine in the spring and should therefore be avoided. The effects on the human body are harmful and abortive: which is why it had always been used to free the bowel of worms, or by women who found themselves with an unwanted pregnancy.

To the Tudors, the cleansing of the bowels after eating fish for a prolonged time was absolutely essential as they were convinced that eating fish came with parasitic intestinal worms. Tansy was also used as a strewing herb to deter flies.

The household accounts of Robert Dudley, Earl of Leicester, show an entry for 'wild tansye' given by Empson in April 1558, and another entry for 'wild tansy and dasye rotes' in May that year, followed by another entry for 'erbes and tanyse' in May. In the spring of 1559, four entries in his household account books show tansy being purchased for the Earl of Leicester.[45]

In Thomas Tusser's *Five Hundred Points of Good Husbandry* from 1573, we find tansy in a list of kitchen herbs and strewing herbs, for the month of March.[46] John Gerard says about the tansy, in his 1597 *Herball*, that in spring the new leaves are mixed with eggs to make tansy cakes. Little does he know about its danger as he goes on to say, that it is pleasant in taste, good for the stomach and clears all bad humors.[47]

TO MAKE A TARTE OF MARIGOLDES, PRYMROSES OR COUSLIPS

Transcribed original recipe

> To make a tarte of borage floures. Take borage floures and perboyle them tender, then strayne them with the yolckes of three or foure egges, and twelfe curdes, or els take three or foure apples, and perboyle withal and strayne them with swete butter and a little mace and so bake it.

To make a tarte of marigolds, prymroses, or couslips. Take the same stuffe to euery of them that you do to the tarte of borage, and the same ceasonynge.

A Proper Newe Booke of Cokerye, 1545/57/75

Modernised version

- ◆ A quantity of fresh, yellow wild primroses (not the coloured ones from the garden centre as those are not edible) Pot marigold, cowslip or borage flowers – boiled, drained and chopped very small
- ◆ 3-4 egg yolks
- ◆ Option 1: One small tub of ricotta cheese
- ◆ Option 2: 3-4 apples, peeled, cored and cooked until soft and then drained and mashed
- ◆ A spoon of unsalted butter – melted
- ◆ Mace to your taste
- ◆ Pastry case – homemade or ready bought

Mix all ingredients in a bowl and use a hand blender if you prefer a smooth texture. Fill pastry cases with mixture and bake at medium heat in the oven until golden brown. Remove from oven and decorate with fresh, edible flowers. Serve hot or cold.

The instructions for this recipe are described as 'take the same mixture as for the borage tart and the same seasoning'. I have amended the recipe accordingly.

Additional information

For this recipe, only use cultivated 'wild primrose' (*Primula vulgaris*) as those growing wild are protected under UK Wildlife and Countryside Act 1981(section 13, part 1b). Any other form of primrose (brightly colored varieties) are a distant relative from Asia and contain a chemical by the name of 'primin' which may cause moderate skin reactions and digestive problems.

Primrose appears in a small number of recipes and botanist John Gerard informs us about their 'qualities' or '*vertues*', which are dry and hot. He further recommends primrose leaves and flowers boiled in water with rose and betony water and then added sugar, pepper, salt and butter.

The flower's name is derived from the Italian for 'first flower in spring'.

FOR SOPPES ON THE FISH DAYES

Transcribed original recipe

> For soppes on the fish days
> TAKE some Onions and frye them with Butter a while: then take Water Pepper and Salte, and put altogeather into a pot with the Butter and Onions, and let them simper vpon the fier. And so serue them vpon soppes, and cast a fewe small Raisins vpon the soppes, and put the broth vpon them.

The VVidowes Treasure, 1588 edition, John Partridge

Modernised recipe

◆ 1 small onion per person, chopped
◆ Butter to fry
◆ Pepper & salt to taste
◆ One slice of toast per person
◆ Some raisins for decoration

Fry the onion in the butter and when golden brown, add a little water, salt and pepper and allow to simmer for a few minutes until the water has evaporated. Serve the onion mixture on toast and sprinkle some raisins on top.

Additional information

Onion was very common in Tudor England but was also strongly associated with the lower classes. One purchase entry in 1564 for onions by the rich London Drapers' Company supports this notion as 12d were spent on 'onions to make porridge for poor folks.'[48]

Onions were classified as 'gross' or 'crass' without today's connotations of disgusting but describing solid, sustaining food only suited for physically very active people.

In Tudor terms, onions required a liquid medium to render them more nourishing. Thus, roasting an onion would make them drier and bitter. This knowledge often helps to explain the use of water in the preparation of a dish (as this recipe) where the use of such makes no sense to improve the taste but explains the balancing efforts of the humors.

The Tudor physician Andrew Boorde observed, that 'they maketh a mans apetyde good, and putteth away fastydyousnes'.

FFOR TARTE OWT OF LENTE (CHEESE PIE)

Transcribed original recipe

> Take neshe chese and pare hit and grynd hit yn A morter and beke eggez and do ther to and then put yn buttur and crème and mell all well to gethur put not to moche butter ther yn if the chese be fatte make a coffin of dowe and close hit a bove with dowe and collor hit a bove with the yolkes of eggs and bake hit well and serue hit furth.

Gentyll manly Cokere (MS Pepys 1047), c.1500

Modernised recipe

- 1 cup cheese (curd cheese, quark or ricotta: 'neshe' = soft)
- Some cream, enough to turn the soft cheese into a very creamy texture
- 1 egg for mixture, one for glazing top
- Seasoning (nutmeg, mace, pepper, ginger, galingale etc) all to taste
- Short crust pastry (ready-made or homemade)

Mix ingredients to form a paste. Grease and flour pastry dish. Line pastry tart case with pastry, leaving enough for a lid. Mix cheese and other ingredients into a thick paste. Fill pie case with cheese mixture. Cover with pastry lid. Glaze with a whisked egg. Bake at medium heat for about 40 minutes or until golden brown.

Additional information

This recipe dates to the reign of Henry VII and in terms of pastry, the '*coffin*' (pastry case) predates the fine paste used towards the end of the end of the century.

Cogan calls cheese 'unwholesome'. New cheese, according to him, is cold in its humoral make up and old, hard cheese best used in 'coffers' or grated into pottages of gammon or bacon. If you must eat cheese, he advises, go for Banbury cheese from Oxfordshire and eat little in quantity at the end of a meal. He observes that other people might prefer well-made cheese from Cheshire (Nantwich) or any other cheese-producing region. His ideal cheese should be: 'not white as snowe is, nor ful of eyes as Argos was, nor olde as Mathusalem was, nor full of whey or weeping as Marie Magdalen was, nor rough as Esau was, nor full of spots as Lazarus.'[49]

In the household of the nobility and gentry cheese wavered between tolerance and disdain. Clearly there were people in the affluent society that enjoyed the taste of cheese and were not put off by all the health warnings. As so often, if a food item had to be imported it became fashionable, trendy and desirable. In August 1537 Cromwell received a present of a dozen Picardy cheeses from John Worth, which he apparently much enjoyed.[50]

TO MAKE STUED POTTAGE IN LENT

Transcribed original recipe

> Take a faire pot, and fil it full of water, and take a saucer full of Oyle Olive, and put it into the pot: then set your pot on the fire and let it boyle. Then take Parslie rootes, and Fennell roots, and scrape them cleane, then cut them of the bignesse of a Prune, and put them into the pot. Then take bread, and cut it in sops and cast it into a pot of wine: then straine it and put it in the pot. Then take Rosemarie, Time, and Parseley, and bind them together, and put them into the pot: then take Dates, Prunes, Corrans, and greate Raisons, and wash them cleane, and put them in the pot. Then season your pot

with Salt, Cloves, Mace, and a little Sugar. If it be not red ynough, take Saunders, and colour your pot therewith, looke that your broth be thicke enough.

The Good Huswifes Handmaide for the Kitchin, 1594 edition

Modernised recipe

- 1 cup of olive oil
- 2 fennel roots, cut into cubes
- 1-2 slices of stale or toasted bread, cut into cubes
- 1 cup of wine
- A bundle of fresh rosemary, thyme and parsley (tied together)
- Handful of dates, prunes, raisins and currants
- Salt, ground cloves, mace and sugar to taste
- Red food colour (to replace saunders) – optional

Boil the vegetables in water with the oil and wine. Add the dried fruit and tie the herbs into a bundle before adding it to the pot. Season the pottage and allow to cook until all roots are soft. Remove herbs and serve the pottage on toast.

Additional information

Saunders or *sanders* is the timber of red sandalwood, from which a red dye is obtained. It is likely to be okay if consumed in small quantities, but I have used food colour instead.

Parsley root is no longer commercially available as it is known to contain fairly high levels of myristicin which can cause hallucinations and severe digestive problems.

'TO SEETH A BREAME'

Transcribed original recipe

> To seeth a Breame. Put White Wine into a pot and let it seeth, then take and cut your Breame in the middest, and put him into the pot: then take an, Onion and chop it small, then take Nutmegs beaten, Synamon and Ginger, whole Mace + a pound of Butter, and let it boyle altogether and so season it with salt, serve it upon sops, and garnish it with fruit.

The Good Huswifes Handmaide for the Kitchin, 1594 edition

Modernised recipe

- ◆ Fresh bream or 2 fillets
- ◆ 500ml white wine
- ◆ 1 -2 onions, chopped
- ◆ Ground nutmeg, cinnamon, ginger to taste
- ◆ 1 whole blade of mace
- ◆ Butter, to your taste
- ◆ A slice of toasted bread per person
- ◆ Some dried fruit for decoration (raisins)

Bring the wine to boil in a pot. Add the fillets or deboned and halved bream. Add the other ingredients and after a few minutes when the fish is cooked, carefully remove it from the pot and serve it on a slice of toasted bread. Decorate with raisins and, if you wish, pour some of the cooking fluid over the fish.

The original recipe uses a very large amount (1lb) of butter. I have reduced the amount significantly.

Additional information

Bream is the common name of a freshwater fish which has been mentioned in Chaucer's *Canterbury Tales* and in the Acts of Parliament of Henry VIII's reign (Act 31; 1539), but it cannot be ruled out that some of the recipes listing bream are referring to the 'Sea Bream' as mentioned by John Russel in *Babees Book* of c.1475.[51]

Bream was considered one of the healthier freshwater species because of the great exercise they get by swimming through fast, rocky currents. The delicate, white flesh was suggested to be easier to digest and contained 'fewer superfluous excrements'[52] and Cogan praises the bream as wholesome. King Philip of Spain was served bream on one of his short stays visiting his wife, Mary, Queen of England.[53]

(ANOTHER) SALLET WITH SALMON & VIOLETS

Transcribed original recipe

> Salmon cut long waies, with slices of onions laid vpon it, and vpon that to cast violets, oyle and vinegar.

The Second Part of the Good Hus-wiues Jewell, 1597
By Thomas Dawson

Modernised recipe

- ◆ Salmon steaks (1 per person)
- ◆ 1 fresh cut onion
- ◆ Olive oil & vinegar
- ◆ Fresh violets or heartsease flowers for decoration
- ◆ Salt & pepper to taste

Briefly dry fry pre-cut onion rings. Fry or grill salmon steaks. Make dressing from olive oil and vinegar (add a little sugar, salt and pepper if you prefer). Serve salmon steaks on a bed of onions and drizzle with dressing. Decorate with fresh violets (from your garden) or use heartsease flowers instead.

Additional information

This recipe makes the ideal picnic or BBQ dish. Violets were classified as 'cold and moist' herbs in Tudor England. Thomas Muffet advises that violets are sometimes used in broths, pottage, 'farrings, sawces, salads and tansies; yet no nourishment is gotten by them, or at the least so little, that they need not, nor ought not to be counted amongst nourishments'.

(ANOTHER) 'SALLET FOR FISH DAY' (HERRING)

Transcribed original recipe

Take pickeeld herring cut long waies and lay them in rundles with onions and parsley chopped, and other herringes the bones being taken out to bee chopped together and laide in the roundles with a long péece laide betwixt the rundles like the proportion of a snake, garnished with Tawney long cut, with vinegar and oile.

The Second Part of the Good Hus-wiues Jewell, 1597, Thomas Dawson

Modernised recipe

- ◆ A jar of pickled herring
- ◆ Fresh onion, chopped
- ◆ Fresh parsley, chopped
- ◆ Some tuna fish for decoration (optional)
- ◆ Some olive oil and vinegar (dressing)

Arrange the pickled herring fillets in circles on your serving dish. Sprinkle with parsley and onion. If you like, you can arrange the fish circles in the shape of a snake and decorate the serving dish with some tuna (flakes). Sprinkle the dish with olive oil and vinegar.

Additional information

Tawney is a sixteenth-century term for tuna. Herring and cod were the most important fish in sixteenth-century Europe. Pickled herring provided several cities facing the North Sea and Baltic with this extremely lucrative trade. Muffet calls herrings a usual and common meat 'coveted as much of the Nobility for variety and wantoness, as used of poor men for want of other provision'. He goes on to say, that pickled herrings are the worst of all but that they can be corrected with salt, pepper and oil.

TO DRESSE A PLAICE

Transcribed original recipe

> It would be boiled with a little parsley, and it is also good fried, putting on it the iuice of Orenges.

Epulario, 1598

Modernised recipe

- ◆ 1 fresh plaice
- ◆ Olive oil, enough to fry the fish
- ◆ 1 orange, the juice of

Heat the olive oil in a frying pan and fry the fish on both sides until done. Serve with orange juice sprinkled on top.

This recipe suggests that you also boil the fish in water with some parsley. However, I have decided to go for the second variant and fried the plaice. I chose olive oil as the recipe is Italian in origin and olive oil was the prime oil used for cooking in Italy.

Additional information

During Henry VIII's time, plaice was so abundant that on the Cornish coast at low tide in some seasons they could be scooped up by the handfuls close in shore.[54]

The average price for plaice between 1522-1543 was 1/2d per pound, making it cheaper than haddock. Moufet, was a big fan of plaice and stated that 'if we had plenty of such wholesome fish, butchers' meat would go begging'.

TO BAKE A TROUT

Transcribed original recipe

To bake Breame, Trout, Mullets, Pike or any fishe. Let them be well seasoned with Cloues, and Mace, Salt and pepper, and so bake them with small Currants Vergis and butter, great raisons and prunes.

The VVidowes Treasure, 1588 edition, John Partridge

Modernised recipe

- ◆ 1 trout fillet per person
- ◆ Pastry to use as an authentic cookery vessel (optional)
- ◆ Ground cloves, mace, salt & pepper to taste
- ◆ Handful of currants, raisins and chopped prunes
- ◆ A little apple vinegar (verjuice, vergis)
- ◆ A little butter

Place fish filets on the pastry or place into an oven dish with a lid. Season with spices and splash a little vinegar on top. Add a little butter and sprinkle the dried fruit over the fish. Close up pastry or lid. Bake in the oven at medium heat until fish is cooked (around 40 minutes to 1½ hours).

Additional information

Fresh water fish from rivers such as trout were considered healthier and better than fish from ponds or a moat as we can see from Andrew Boorde's comment: 'The fysshe the whiche is in ryuers and brokes be more holsomer than they the which be in pooles, pondes, or mootes, or any other standynge waters; for they doth laboure'

TO FRY WHITING

Transcribed original recipe

> First flay them and wash them clean and scale them, that doon, lap them in floure and fry them in Butter and oyle. Then serve them, mince apples or onions and fry them, then put them into a vessel with white wine, vergious, salt, pepper, cloves & mace, and boile them together on the Coles, and serve it upon the Whitings.

A Book of Cookrye, 1591, A.W

Modernised recipe

- ◆ 1 whole whiting or fillets (remove skin first if you prefer)
- ◆ A bowl of flour within which to dust the fish
- ◆ 1-2 apples, peeled and chopped
- ◆ 1 onion, peeled and chopped
- ◆ A little white wine to make up the sauce
- ◆ A spoonful of apple vinegar (vergious)
- ◆ Salt, ground pepper, cloves and mace to taste
- ◆ Olive oil or butter to fry

Fry the onions and the apples in some of the oil (or butter). Add the wine and spices. Allow to cook for a few minutes and remove from the heat. Turn fish in flour and fry in the remaining oil on both sides until done. Serve on a platter and pour apple/onion mixture on top.

Additional information

Whiting are a small member of the cod family. Thomas Muffet states that the best whiting are taken in 'Tweede' and that all physicians recommend them for a light, wholesome and good meal. He also reckons that they are good sodden with salt and thyme and dried after the manner of stockfish.

IF YOU VVILL MAKE GREENE SAUCE ...

Transcribed original recipe

If you vvill make greene sauce looke in the chapter before, vvhere
it is set downe, follpvv the order therein prescribed.

Take Parsley, wild Time, and Mint, with other good hearbes,
adding to t hem Salt, Pepper, and Ginger, beate them together,
and temper it with strong Vinegar, then straine them: and if you
will haue it tast of Garlike, beate some heads of Garlike with it,
as much as you thinke good.

Epulario, 1598

Modernised recipe

- ◆ A handful of very finely chopped parsley, wild thyme and mint
  (plus any other seasonal herbs such as rosemary, sage, etc)
- ◆ Some crushed garlic clove, to your taste
- ◆ Salt, crushed pepper and ground ginger, to your taste
- ◆ A cupful of vinegar

Put all ingredients in a pot and cook for a few minutes until the garlic is soft. Then use a hand blender to purée the sauce or sieve mixture through a muslin cloth to get a green, thin, translucent sauce.

It is not clear from this recipe whether the ingredients were left raw or cooked, but having compared it with similar, contemporary recipes I made the decision to cook it as raw garlic was considered unhealthy. The recipes advice to refer to the chapter before did not supply any further clues either. However, you are free to leave the ingredients uncooked for a fresher, greener sauce which would go well with barbecued fish!

Additional information

Parsley was without any doubt, the most used herb in Tudor England. Andrew Boorde said about parsley in 1542, that 'Parsley is good to breke the stone, and causeth a man to pysse; it is good for the stomacke, & doth cause a man to haue a swete breth'.

Thyme, as acknowledged by Cogan, was a herb much used in the Tudor kitchen. He classifies it as 'hot and dry in the third degree', making it ideal for correcting cold and wet fish.

In 1599 Henry Butts recommends mint in cold weather and for old men. According to him, mint should be eaten sparingly, preferably with cold herbs.

TO MAKE BALLES OF ITALIE

Transcribed original recipe

> Take a peece of a legge of Veale, paboyle it, then pare away all the skin and sinews –and chop the Veale verie small, a little salt and pepper, two yolks of Egges hard rosted, and seven yolkes rawe, temper all these with your Veale, then make balles thereof as big as walnuts, and boyle them in beefe broth, or mutton broth, as ye did the other before rehearsed, and put into your broth ten beaten cloves, a race of Ginger, a little Vergious, foure or five lumpes of marrowe whole, let them stew the space of an hower. Then serve them upon sops, eight or nine in a dish, and betwixt the balles you must lay the lumps of marrow.

> *The Good Huswifes Handmaide for the Kitchin*, 1594 edition

Modernised recipe

- ◆ Approx. 450g minced veal
- ◆ 2 egg yolks, hard boiled and chopped fine
- ◆ 7 raw egg yolks
- ◆ Lamb or beef stock
- ◆ Ground cloves, ginger to taste
- ◆ A few spoonfuls of apple vinegar ('vergious')
- ◆ Some bone marrow (or substitute with suet)
- ◆ Slice of toasted bread per person (sops)

Mix the mincemeat with the hard-boiled eggs and the egg yolks and form balls the size of a walnut. Should they not stick, add some breadcrumbs or flour until they do. Cook the balls in the stock at low heat for about one hour and add the bone marrow or suet and the spices. Put the sops (toasted bread slices) into the bottom of your bowl and serve the balls on top. You may pour some of the stock over the balls and if you opted for bone marrow in the recipe, scoop that out of the bone and decorate the balls with it.

Additional information

English physician Edmund Hollings (1556-1612) was of the opinion that because veal was easy to digest you could eat more of it.[55]

TO MAKE ALLOWES TO ROSTE OR BOILE

Transcribed original recipe

> Take a Leg of mutton and slice it thin, then take out the kidneys of the mutton hauing it minced small, with Isope, time, parsley, & the yolkes of hard egges, then bind it with crumms of white bread and rawe eggs, and put to it proines and great raisons, and for want of them barberies or Goosberies, or grapes seasoning it with Cloues, mace, pepper Sinnamon, ginger & salt. You may make a mugget of a Sheepe as these allowes bee, sauing you must put no mutton into it.

The Second Part of the Good Hus-wiues Jewell, 1597

Modernised recipe

- Steaks of mutton or lamb, flattened
- Kidney, chopped (substitute with some lamb mince if you prefer)
- Handful of chopped hyssop, thyme & parsley
- 3 yolks, hard boiled and chopped
- Handful of breadcrumbs
- 2-3 raw eggs, whisked
- Handful of prunes (chopped), raisins, barberries, gooseberries or grapes
- Ground clovers, mace, pepper, cinnamon, ginger and salt to taste

Lay out your flattened steaks and season them with the spices and salt. Mix all other ingredients together and form little balls, one for each steak. Press those into the steaks, close them up and secure them with cotton string or toothpicks. Bake them in the oven in a lidded dish for about an hour or until done. Alternatively, cook them in some lamb stock at medium heat until done.

Additional information

Aloes are dishes made with sliced meat, often rolled up with an enclosed filling. The term comes from the Old French '*aloe*' for larks (a bird) which they originally imitated. Aloes could also be made of beef.

Interesting here is the choice of two cooking methods: boiled in fluid or roasted over embers. A Tudor cook would have chosen the boiling option for the drier season and for elderly people, as both needed the fluid to counterbalance the hot and dry humors present in both. Winter, on the other hand, and younger people would have required the roasted option to keep them healthy and 'balanced' in their humors.

TO BOYLE YONG PEASON OR BEANS

Transcribed original recipe

First shale them and seethe them in faire water, then take them out of the water and put them into boyling milk, then take the yolks of Egs with crums of bread, and ginger, and straine them thorow a strainer with the said milk, then take chopped percely, Saffron and Salt, and serve it foorth for Pottage.

A Book of Cookrye, 1591

Modernised recipe

- ◆ Fresh young peas, shelled
- ◆ Milk, enough to cover the peas
- ◆ Egg yolks, 2 per person
- ◆ Breadcrumbs, enough to achieve a nice smooth texture
- ◆ Ground ginger, to taste
- ◆ Fresh parsley, finely chopped
- ◆ 1-2 strands saffron, crushed
- ◆ Salt, to taste

Boil the peas very briefly in a little water. Drain and put back into pot. Add milk to just cover peas and allow to boil up. Add remaining ingredients except for parsley, saffron and salt. Just add enough breadcrumbs to thicken the texture of the pottage. Use a blender or push mixture through a sieve. Add parsley, saffron and salt. Serve hot.

Additional information

Peas were among the few vegetables which had no social stigma attached to them and therefore were eaten by both the poor and the rich.

However, in 1587 William Harrison draws attention to the relevance of the contemporary proverb: 'Hunger setteth his first foot into the horse manger,' and by that he refers to the need of the poor to use pea and bean flour as he bemoans the inability of the working class to afford bread made from wheat or rye.[56]

For most of Tudor England, only the field grown peas were known – left on the plant until they had naturally dried and then cooked in thick stews such as pease pottage. Only in the sixteenth century was a distinction made between the field grown and the garden peas. Field grown peas had colourful flowers and small pods, garden peas mostly white flowers and bigger seeds. One of the varieties of 'Tudor peas' still available are the so-called Carlin or 'pigeon' peas.

In 1599 Henry Butts recommends the new, tender peas for the hot seasons and provides us with their humoral qualities: cold in first degree and temperately moist. His recommendation in their culinary use is to dress them well with almond oil, salt, pepper and the 'iuyce of sower hearbes'.

There was a general consensus among contemporary physicians that legumes, including peas, were 'gross, windy and hard to digest'. While it was believed that peas were safer than beans for the stomachs of the affluent.

The practice of eating peas green and immature (petit pois), arrived fairly late in England. There is one recipe in the English translation of Epulario from 1598 which appears to suggest that the peas were used still in the green, in their husk.

What made vegetables attractive in Renaissance court circles was their novelty in terms of new varieties of traditional plants or their rarity in being served up at unusual times of the year.

HOW TO MAKE SAUSAGES

Transcribed original recipe

> Take the Fillets of a Hogge, and halfe as muche of the suet of the Hogge: and choppe them both very small, then take grated bread, two or three yolkes of egges a spoonful of groce pepper, as much salt, temper them with a little creame, and so put them into the skinnes and broyle thé on a gridiorne.

The Good Hous-wiues Treasurie, 1588, anonymous

Modernised recipe

- ◆ 2kg of pork fillet, finely minced
- ◆ 1kg of suet, finely minced
- ◆ 60-80g breadcrumbs
- ◆ 1tbsp pepper
- ◆ 1tbsp of salt
- ◆ 3 yolks
- ◆ Approx.. 100ml double cream
- ◆ Sausage skins

Mix all the ingredients and press the mass into sausage skins. Tie them closed. Cut into individual sausages. If you know a friendly butcher, they might be happy to put your sausage meat into the skins for you.

Additional information

Although in medieval times sausages had formed part of the diet of merchants and people from the financially better off lower class, they were seldom found at the table of the English gentry until the early modern period.[57]

In 1522, on Ash Wednesday, the Reformation in Zürich (Switzerland) started when a group of evangelical believers defied the rules of Lenten abstinence by cooking and consuming sausages.

Sausages usually take centre stage in carnivalesque celebrations, being the symbol of not only gustatory but sexual license. Sausages were seen as notorious symbols of male sexuality, masculinity in general and the common man. In an engraving by Pieter van der Heyden, based on Pieter Bruegel the Elder's drawings and titled *The Fat Kitchen* (1563), sausages are displayed in abundance symbolizing insatiable appetite and lust. In several illustrations from the late 1500s mock battles between fat men holding sausages and fighting a thin woman holding a fish (Lady Lent) is a recurring theme representing the religious conflicts between sausage and meat-eating Protestants and the fasting Catholics at Lent.

Chapter 2

SUMMER

Food in Summer

In Tudor England, June, July and August were the months of plenty and fresh produce was in abundance. It comes as no surprise that this is the season when the Tudors contemplated being tempted by fresh, raw fruit and other food believed to be very watery and helpful in cooling down the body in the summer heat.

July is the month when people in Tudor England would have been able to pick fresh strawberries, cherries, plums and gooseberries. Only strawberries and cherries were eaten fresh; plums and gooseberries appear to have been cooked before consumption. It is safe to assume that raspberries were enjoyed fresh too, but there are no original accounts to confirm this.

The Tudors were a little hesitant in eating fresh or 'raw', uncooked berries as well as 'watery' vegetables such as cucumber and salad leaves, as their assigned cold and wet properties made them potentially dangerous to eat. However, this could be corrected by cooking them, adding hot and dry spices or simply by eating them on a hot and dry day, which would cure the shortcomings.

Summer was also time for enjoying unsalted, fresh meat which was much welcome after months of eating very salty preserved produce. This was the season to prepare for the forthcoming winter and so it was a very busy time, not just to harvest but also preserve foodstuffs.

Elyot defines the period of summer from the eighth of May to the eighth of August.[1]

Thomas Cogan explains how to eat well in the summer in his publication *The Haven of Health*. He strongly advises against eating too much meat in the summer as it is 'hurtfull' and that it is best to eat little and often, as *Galen* taught. Meat should be boiled rather than roasted and pottage or broths made from 'cold herbs' such as lettuce, endive, chicory and violet leaves were most wholesome. Unsurprisingly, he also encourages to drink more – 'wine allayed with water' – for people with too hot complexions (mostly young men), while those with too cold complexions (mostly elderly women) should naturally drink less.[2]

Picnics and al fresco dining in Tudor England

People have always enjoyed eating outdoors on a warm summer's day, but it was the sixteenth century that took eating outdoors to new heights. The banquet in the garden was a distinctively Tudor social institution that began at the highest level at court and soon filtered down as a new fashion for all well-to-do families in England. This fashion spread rapidly down the social scale and took the hearts of the English by storm.

Its popularity was aided by the increased quantity of sugar that became available in England and the introduction of the banqueting house – a place specifically designed for eating portable banqueting food in a pleasant but private surrounding away from the main house.

Banqueting houses arose from the growing desire for more privacy and less ceremony. Eating in a purpose-built house in the garden away from the prying eyes of servants in a romantic setting appealed to the Tudors as much as it does to us. Banqueting food served in such places could easily be transported there and servants dismissed entirely. The food was intended to be eaten cold and often was of an aphrodisiac nature. For the perfect location, a viewpoint with a vista, built at an elevation giving deep spiritual and physical pleasure, was paramount. The sounds of birdsong, splashing water mixed with the fragrance of flowers and spring air was to refresh the mind and stimulate lust, much aided by sugary treats and spiced drinks.

The renaissance garden idea was to represent paradise on earth, where senses, intellect and spirit were enhanced. Banquet food served in the garden was food for the mind and its taste heightened the sense of reality. The very nature of the banquet in the garden was not to satisfy the stomach but to delight the eye and all other senses.

Food also featured in annual outdoor celebrations, much enjoyed by the common people. Country people gathered at various festivals that filled the calendar, many of which were accompanied by abundant eating and drinking outdoors. Agricultural labourers sometimes took hearty meals in the fields, especially at busy times of the year, as suggested by Pieter Bruegel the Elder's 'Harvesters' at the MET in New York. These breaks also offered a chance to sit and talk and enjoy the warm weather in pleasant company.

Hunting parties took breaks to refuel for later pursuits and a late-sixteenth-century woodcut by George Tuberville from 1575 provides us with a good insight into what sort of picnic food was provided. Several recipes from this period provide food suitable for picnics: all kinds of pies, tarts, jellies, salads and 'cold meat'.

Brigitte Webster, with kind permission by NT Lacock Abbey. Photo showing banquet table at Lacock Abbey.

We are extremely lucky in that several locations showing such unique places of Tudor banqueting have survived for us to visit. Sir William Sharington's banqueting tower at Lacock Abbey in Wiltshire was built between 1549-53 and still features the original banqueting furniture in Italianate design inside the octagonal lookout tower comprising two banqueting rooms.

Herbs in the Tudor kitchen

To the Tudors, 'Herbes' included not just our commonly known herbs but also green, leafy vegetables such as kale, cabbage and lettuce. Herbs were highly esteemed for their many purposes: pot herbs in the kitchen to flavour meals, medicinal herbs to treat medical issues and sweet herbs were used for strewing on the floor to serve as a kind of room freshener.

Andrew Boorde, English monk, physician and traveller said in his book *Dyetary of Helth*, published in 1542, 'There is no herb, nor weed, but God have given virtue to them, to help man, but for as much as Pliny, macer and Diascorides, with many other old ancient and appropriate doctors, has written and pertracted of their virtues, I therefore now will write no further of herbs, but will speak of other matters that shall be more necessary.'[3] 'Virtues' in Tudor terms can be understood as health benefits, and in line with this the Tudors also ascribed the so called humoral 'properties' to the nature of all herbs. For a cold and wet country like England one needed herbs with 'hot' and 'dry' properties to balance the humors and to stay healthy. However, 'cold' and 'wet' properties were actively needed to bring down a temperature or to stay cool on a hot summer's day.

Most herbs in England such as borage, caraway, coriander, cumin, fennel, lovage, lemon balm, mint, parsley, anise, garden thyme, pot marigold and chervil were introduced by the Romans. By 1200 hyssop had arrived, and by 1300 lavender, sweet marjoram and sweet rocket were known. Basil was probably introduced between 1300 and 1400 and so was rosemary and English-grown saffron. Summer and winter savory as well as sweet cicely first appeared during the Tudor age. Bay tree (laurel) was first mentioned in 1562, dyer's chamomile in 1561 and licorice in 1562.

Thomas Tusser, author of the *Five Hundred Points of Good Husbandry*, published in 1573/77, lists in his 'March Abstract' the following herbs for the kitchen: avens, betony, beets, bloodwort, bugloss, burnet, borage, cabbage, clary, coleworts, cresses, endive, fennel, French mallows, French saffron, lang de beef, leeks, lettuce, longwort, liverwort, marigolds, mercury, mints, nep, onions, orache, patience, parsley, penny-royal, primrose, poret, rosemary, sage, English saffron, summer savory, sorrel, spinach, siethes, tansy, thyme violets.

For 'sallads' and sauce he recommends the following herbs: alexanders, artichokes, blessed thistle, cucumbers and cresses.[4]

Many of these herbs we no longer use for culinary purposes and some we simply regard as 'weed'. Others are now defined as vegetables rather than herbs and some we avoid all together because they are now considered poisonous (e.g., rue, tansy)

Before the reformation, monasteries were the centre for the cultivation of all herbs. After the closure of all monasteries, it was up to people with access to a little land to take over and many people started growing herbs in their own small gardens. People still continued to collect herbs in the wild, but for convenience herb gardens were established near kitchens. Manor houses and the nobility would also often receive herbs from the common people as a gift. In Robert Dudley, Earl of Leicester's account book of 1558, there are a number of entries for 'erbes' being given such as 'Lesam's daughter bringing your lordship erbes', for which she was rewarded 2s.[5]

According to John Partridge in his *The Treasurie of Commodious Conceits,* first published in 1573, 'Herbes should be gathered when they be full of Sappe, and ere they shrink'. He also advises, that 'Hearbes that growth in the Feldes' are better than those that 'growth in Townes, in Gardns, and those that growth on hills in the field be best for Medicines, for commonly they be lesse, & not so fat, and have more virtue.'[6]

Salads in Tudor England

Salads are a prime example of how much it depended on where in Europe you lived in the sixteenth century as people had a very different idea about what salads were and how they prepared them. Platina, in late-fourteenth-century Italy, wrote that salads made a 'light, mild and pleasant' start to the meal, and he described their composition: 'different varieties of lettuce, and herbs such as mint, parsley, chervil, oregano and fennel dressed with salt, oil and vinegar'.

Salads were quite common in the fourteenth and early fifteenth centuries in England, but already by the time Henry VII came to the throne in 1485, they were looked down upon on and considered only good enough for 'hogs and savage beasts to feed upon than mankind', as William Harrison expressed in his *Description of England* from 1587. 'Beware of sallettes & raw fruytes for they will make your soverayne seke' advised Wynkin de Worde in 1508.

According to the Tudor's belief in the humors, raw salad leaves were believed to produce cold and moist humors, which was clearly to be avoided and possibly dangerous in England. However, this could be balanced out with the addition of dry and hot pepper or salt, making it acceptable to eat.

While in Italy and Spain raw salads were appreciated early on, especially in the hot summer months, salads as we know them today were regarded with great suspicion in England. In 1596 the English courtier and Italophile Robert Dallington noted that in Tuscany, 'a sallet is as ordinary as salt at the English table, eaten by all sorts of people and all the year'. In England 'boyled sallets' were the preferred option – boiled vegetables served cold with oil and vinegar.

By the 1540s the English physician Sir Thomas Elyot was recommending herbs like rocket, savory, borage, purslane, and onions along with imported olives and capers. In his book *Castel of Helth* he credited them with 'stirring up the appetite to meat' and 'promoting digestion'. Both very important and desirable in Tudor England.

In the 1550s salads began to be served as a starter at the beginning of the first course at lunchtime and supper. Early salads contained cooked and preserved items as well as fresh ingredients. In the 1580 edition of *Five Hundred Points of Good Husbandry*, catering for the slightly less affluent circles, Thomas Tusser mentions a surprisingly large range of herbs and vegetables to grow for use in 'sallets and sauce': Alexander, artichoke (globe), asparagus, blessed thistle, borage, Burnet, carrot, colewort, cucumber, cress, endive, garlic, hops, leeks, lettuce, mint, mustard, musk-melon, onion, parsley, purslane, radish, rampion (wild garlic), rocket, sage, samphire, scallion (spring onion), sea-holly, skirret, sorrel, sperage, spinach, succory (chicory), tarragon, violets.

By this time the consumption of salads was 'not only resumed among the poor commoners, but also fed upon as dainty dishes at the table to delicate merchants, gentlemen and the nobility, who make their provision yearly for new seeds out of strange countries,' according to country vicar William Harrison. In his *Description of England* (1587), he also bemoans the wealthy's urge to purchase exotic food in favour of home-grown, local, produce and fresh salads. He may also have implied that the English ate salads only in the summer in the following observation: 'I might here take occasion to set down the variety used by antiquity in their beginnings of their diets, wherein almost every nation had a several fashion, some beginning of custom (as we do in summertime) with salads at supper and some ending with lettuce.'

Herbalist John Gerard confirmed in his Herball of 1597, that 'salad is served in these daies in the beginning of supper and eaten first before any other meat ... for being taken before meat it doth many time stir up appetite'. He also observed, that 'if eaten after supper it keepeth away drunkennesse which cometh by the wine'.

Salads came in three categories: simple, compound and grand. The simplest salads were rather basic: freshly gathered and washed salad herbs, lettuce dressed in oil, vinegar and sugar, or boiled onions, asparagus or samphire, cucumbers dressed with oil, vinegar and pepper. Vegetables such as onion, spinach, asparagus, carrots and globe artichoke were first boiled, dressed with vinegar, olive oil and pepper and then served cold.

In the spring, mixed salads were made of the finest young stalks and buds of herbs such as mint, lettuce, violets, marigold and spinach and dressed in vinegar olive oil and sugar.

Compound salads contained a little bit of everything from fresh herbs, cooked and raw vegetables to preserved ingredients.

Grand salads are a feature of the late sixteenth century and developed an impressive appearance. These were huge plates decorated with salad herbs, enriched with nuts, dried fruits, and capers. The salad was then garnished with a riot of colours with edible decorations such as flowers or coloured vinegars. Some vegetables such as carrots and other roots were carved into fancy shapes. The purpose was to impress with taste and looks.

In the sixteenth century, salad dressings are very similar except that lettuces were now included in salads (no longer just boiled) and salt was replaced with sugar. Regular deliveries from the king's royal gardens included lettuce, cucumber and radishes. Cucumber was once transported from Beaulieu in Essex to Hertford for the king's pleasure. Radishes appear only once in the whole list of Privy Purse expenses and may still have been a novelty in the late 1520s.

Olive oil in salads seems to have been a rich person's taste adopted from the Continent in the beginning of the sixteenth century and it gradually spread among the gentry. Vinegar came in numerous possible flavours according to the fruits or plants inserted in the liquid. The English word vinegar comes from French 'vinaigre' meaning 'sour wine'. Vinegar was the universal seasoning, widely available and cheap. Verjuice (agrestum/agraz) is a slightly fermented juice of sour green apples, or better, crab apples or unripe grapes.

Recipes

TO MAKE UINEGAR OF ROSES (VIOLETS & ELDERFLOWERS)

Transcribed original recipe

In Sommer time when Roses blowe, gather them ere they be full spred or blowne out, and in dry wether: plucke the leaues, let them lye halfe a day vpon a fayre borde, then haue a vessel with Uineger of one or two gallons (if you wyll make so much roset,) put therein a great quantity of the sayd leaues, stop the vessel close after that you haue styrrwd them wel together, let it stand a day and a night, then deuide your Uineger & Rose leaues together in two parts put thein two great Glasses & put in Rose leaues ynoughe, stop the Glasses close, set them vpon a Shelfe vnder a wall syde, on the Southside wtout your house where the Sonne may come to them the most parte of the daye, let them stande there all the whole Somer longe: and then strayne the vinegar from the Roses, and keepe the vinegre. If you shall once in .x. days, take and strain out Rose leaues, and put in newe leaues of halfe a days gathering, the vyneger wyll haue the more flauor and odour of the Rose.

You may vse in steede of Uinegre, wyne: that it may wexe eyfre, and receiue ye virtue of the Roses, both at once. Moreouer,

you may make your vinegar of wine white, red or claret, but the red doth most binde the bellie, & white doth most lose. Also the Damaske Rose is not so great a binder as the red Rose, and the white Rose loose the most of all: wereof you may make vinegre roset. Thus also, you may make Uinegre of Uiolets, or of Elder flowers: but you must first gather & vse your flowers of Eldern, as shalbe shewed hereafter, when we speake of making Conserue of Elderne flowers.

The Treasurie of Commodious Conceits, 1573 edition, John Partridge

Modernised recipe

- ◆ Handful of rose petals (Violet flowers or Elderflower)
- ◆ 250ml white wine vinegar

Collect the flowers (petals) when in full bloom on a dry day. Fill up a glass jar with vinegar and add the flowers. Close the lid and leave to stand in the sun for a few days. Remove flowers and replace with fresh ones. Leave to stand for the summer or until the vinegar is taking on the colour of the flowers. Use to decorate grilled meat, fish or in salads.

Additional information

In Tudor England, vinegar was an extremely important ingredient in food, with many different flavours according to the fruits or plants inserted in the basic liquid, verjuice. Verjuice was stored in barrels and often produced by farmers and then sold. The flavour and colour could be changed by adding cloves and gillyflowers, violets, rose petals, elder flowers, cowslips, primroses, broom flowers, hawthorn flowers, berries, raisins, gooseberries, or pears. The season for making verjuice was the autumn but flavouring them with flowers was done in the spring.

Early in the Tudor period, vinegar was used to produce sweet and sour sauces for meat and fish, but towards the end of the Tudor period this gave way to new ways of making sauces and introduced a new fashion: cooked, cold salads and those demanded all sort of fancy coloured and flavoured vinegars.

It has also had a fair use as a remedial food and acted as a primary 'corrective' to foods of the wrong humoral properties. Henry Butts classified vinegar as 'cold in the first and moyst in the second degree'. He advises to take vinegar with raisons of the sun, and in his opinion the most desirable vinegar is made from the best wine, one year old and is 'bettered by putting Roses in it'. Cogan is the only Tudor physician who points out that vinegar helps with slimming.

Vinegar could be purchased ready-made from spice shops, markets or farmers. The Register of Thetford Priory for the financial year of 1524/5 shows a sum of 2s 6d paid for 'vynegyr'.[7] The household accounts of Kenninghall Palace in Norfolk in the year of 1525 show an entry of 4-4½d per gallon of vinegar.[8]

TO MAKE ALL KINDE OF SYROPS

Transcribed original recipe

> Take Buglosse, Borage, white Endiue, of each .i. handful, of Rosemary, Tyme, Isop, winter Sauery, of each halfe a handful sseth them (being fyrste broken between your' hands) in .iii. quarters of water, vnto iii. Pints, the straine it, and put to ye liquor, whole cloues an ounce, pouder of Cinimon: half an ounce, pouder of Ginger: a quarter of an ounce .i. Nutmeg in powder, of

suger half a pound, or more: let them seethe vpon a softe fyre well styred for burning too, vntyll it come to thicknesse ofliue Hony, then keepe it in Gallypots, if you put i. pynte Malmzey in second seething, it wyl be better. When it is perfecte, haue sixe graynes of fine Muske in powder, stiffe it amongst your Syrop as ye put it in the Gallypot, and couer it.

This Syrop will last many yeres and is excellent against swowning and faitnesse of hert it coforteth the Brayne and Sinewes, if it bee vsed as muche as a Hasell Nut at once, at your pleasure.

The Treasurie of Commodious Conceits, 1573, John Partridge

Modernised recipe

- ◆ Handful of lettuce
- ◆ Handful of other green leafy herb such as spinach, etc.
- ◆ Handful of borage leaves (or similar)
- ◆ ½ handful of fresh rosemary
- ◆ ½ handful of fresh thyme

- ½ handful of fresh hyssop
- ½ handful of fresh winter savory
- ¾ pint of water
- 1oz whole cloves
- ½oz ground cinnamon
- ¼oz ground ginger
- One ground nutmeg
- ½lb sugar (or more if preferred – I added an extra 250g)
- 1 pint of Madeira wine (optional)

Slightly rub all herbs in your hands and then add to water. Boil for a few minutes (until water starts absorbing flavour and colour from herbs). Strain through a sieve and add the spices to the remaining liquid. Add Madeira wine if desired. Bring to boil again and let it gently cook until the consistency is similar to honey. Allow to cool, add a few drops of 'musk flavored' oil if you prefer and pour into a jar or earthenware pot. I did not have any bugloss (Alkanet) in my garden, so I just replaced with an extra measure of lettuce.

Additional information

The Tudors used syrups as a medicinal substance and as such did not dilute then with water. As the recipe claims, this syrup was considered good for the brain and the sinus and you only needed to take as little as the size of a hazelnut whenever you felt like it.

Cordials and syrups were both held in high regard as medicine and were therefore not used as a drink. It was the arrival of cheaper sugar from the Americas during Elizabeth's reign which fuelled a fashion in the creation of diverse flavoured cordials and syrups as sugar in itself was seen as a magical cure for many ailments.

Musk is a type of aromatic substance commonly used as base in perfumery. It includes glandular secretions from the musk deer and it was commonly added to food in sixteenth- and seventeenth-century England. I used a musk alternative (musk flavoured oil).

Recipe books from Tudor England often list culinary recipes together with medicinal recipes and then as now it was understood that food in itself was a kind of medicine provided by nature.

In William Turner's entry of lettuce in *The Names of Herbes*, he suggests that there are three kinds: endive, cabbage and spinach.[9] John Gerard states in 1597 that the leaves and flowers of borage put into wine make men and women glad and merry. He also mentions that syrup made from the flowers comforts the heart and that the flowers are used in salads to make the mind glad.[10] Rosemary was generally used in the kitchen for flavouring pottages and it also features as an ingredient in cordials.

The Tudors are the first to mention winter and summer savory and John Gerard lists both. They are considered hot and dry in the third degree, which is good, and, even better, it 'maketh thin' – slimming world Tudor style. He advises to eat it with beans and peas and other 'windie pulses'.

PICKLED SAMPHIRE SALLAD WITH OIL & VINEGAR OR USED AS SAUCE

Transcribed original recipe

> The leaues kept in pickle, and eaten in sallads with oile and vinegar, is a pleasant sauce for meat, wholesome for the stoppings of the liuer, milt, kidneies and bladder: it prouoketh vrine gently, it openeth the stoppings of the intrals, and stirreth vp an appetite to meat.

'Herball', 1597, John Gerard

Modernised recipe

- ◆ Pickled samphire (boil in a wine/vinegar mix with salt until soft and allow to 'mature' in a closed pickle jar for a week to absorb the flavour)
- ◆ Olive oil and mild vinegar to taste

Take your pickled samphire and mix it with some olive oil and mild apple vinegar. Blend into a smooth paste and serve with grilled meat or fish.

Additional information

In 1548 Samphire is first being mentioned in England as part of William Turner's *The Names of Herbes* where he says about it: 'Crithmus named also crithamus & Batis is called in englishe Sampere, it is named of some Herbaries creta marina, it growth much in rockes & cliffs beside Douer.'[11]

Originally *sampiere*, a corruption of the French 'Saint Pierre' (Saint Peter), was named after the patron saint of fishermen because all of the original plants with its name grow in rocky, salt-sprayed regions along the coast of northern Europe or in its coastal marsh areas. There are two kinds, the rock samphire and the marsh samphire (glasswort, *Salicornia Europea*).

Samphire once grew freely along parts of the coast and in particular in East Anglia where it still survives in some parts. The garden grown variety lacks the pronounced salty characteristic of the wild plant.

Samphire featured prominently during the winter season in local diets in the Elizabethan period and was sufficiently well known to become a commercial product. Historically, it was usually pickled with sea salt and vinegar and eaten as an appetite stimulant and as a condiment to meat. Barrels of pickled samphire were procured by Sir William Petre at Ingatestone (Essex). Joan Thirsk, in her publication of *Food in Early Modern England*, suggests that the references to samphire from 1580 onwards may well refer to a growing localised business.[12]

The fifteenth-century herbal *Der Gart der Gesundheit* specifies samphire as 'warm' and 'dry' in the second degree.[13] In his *Haven of Health*, Thomas Cogan confirms John Gerard's description on how it was prepared: 'Sampere is of much like nature, and used as a sawce with meats after the same manner: It is a weed growing neare to the Sea side, and is very plentifull about the Ile of Man, from whence it is brought to divers parts of England, preserved in Brine & is no lesse wholesome than Capers.'[14]

SALLET FOR FISH DAYS – SALSIFY OR SKIRRET, 1597

Transcribed original recipe

> Skirret rootes cut long waies in a dish with tawney long cutte, vinegar and Oyle.

The second Part of the Good Hus-wiues Jewell, Thomas Dawson

Modernised recipe

- Skirret roots or salsify roots (pictured)
- Tuna (or tawney) steak grilled and cut into long strips or tinned flakes
- Vinegar, olive oil

Clean the roots, peel them and quickly put them into boiling water to prevent them from oxidizing and turning brown. Cook until tender. Drain and dress with vinegar and oil, decorating the dish with tuna.

Additional information

Both skirret (also known as water parsnip), and salsify (sometimes known as goatsbeard or 'Go to bed at noone') are old root vegetables and do occur in the wild.

Salsify does not really appear in Tudor recipes, but we know from other contemporary sources that it was consumed. John Gerard gives us some hints on how to prepare it in his 'Herball' of 1597/1633: 'The roots of Goats-beart boiled in wine and drunk, assuage the pain and prickling stitches of the sides. The same boiled in water until they be tender and buttered as Parsneps and carrots, are most pleasant and wholesome meat, in delicate taste far surpassing either Parsnep or Carrot, which meat procures appetite and strengthens those that have been sick for a long lingering disease.'

Skirret, the other root vegetable, has a fairly similar appearance but different leaves and appears a lot more often in Tudor recipes. The English name is derived from the Middle English 'skirwort' meaning white root. The plant originates from China but arrived in Europe by or before Roman times. By the sixteenth century, John Gerard states that its humors are hot and dry.[15] *The Forme of Cury* (1390) includes the earliest English recipes with 'skyrwates'. In 1548 William Turner compares the parsnip with its relative, the skirret.[16]

Thomas Moffet, describes various culinary ways to use skirret: 'usually they are boild till they be tender, and then eaten cold with vinegar, oil and pepper; but if they be roasted four or five together in a wet paper under embers or strain'd into tart-stuff, and so baked with sugar, butter, and rosewater.'

FOR SPINAGE, 1588 EDITION

Transcribed original recipe

> Take Spinage and washe it well, then laye it vpon a boorde and giue it fiue or six choppers with a knife, then put it into a frying panne with a little faire water and seethe it well, then take Butter, Vergis and Salte, and put it to the Spinage, and so boyle it together in a pot or between two Platters: and so serue them out with Soppes.

The VVidowes Treasure, John Partridge

Modernised recipe

- ◆ Fresh spinach, washed and finely chopped
- ◆ A little butter for frying
- ◆ Vinegar and salt, to taste
- ◆ A slice of toasted white bread (sop) per person

Cook the spinach in a little salted water until soft but take care not to overcook it. Drain the spinach and transfer it to a pan with the butter. Give it a quick fry and add some mild vinegar. Put the slice of toast on a plate and pile the spinach mixture on top. Garnish with some fresh edible flowers if you like and serve hot. This is a classic example of a 'boiled' salad.

Additional information

Spinach arrived in Europe sometime in the late medieval period via the Moors who had occupied Spain. Henry Butts (1575-1632) informs us in his *Dyets dry dinner* that spinach is fried in its own juice without water and then improved with the addition of oil, sorrel juice and raisins of the sun.

Thomas Moffett states that 'Spinache being boiled soft and then eaten with butter, small currens and sugar heat together upon a chafing dish, giveth no bad nor little nourishment to dried bodies, and is onley hurtful to such as be over-phlegmatick.'

Thomas Cogan states that spinach is being used in broths and pottages and apparently helps with backache.

SPINAGE (FRITTERS), 1588 EDITION

Transcribed original recipe

> TAKE Spinage and parboyle it well, then wringe the liquor cleane from it then choppe it very small, and put it into a Platter and breake some Egges into it: then take a handfull of grated bread and put into it and suger with a little salte, and beate all this together but let it not be too thicke nor to thinne, but better thicke then thinne: then take a frying panne with some Butter, and when the Butter is a little more then melted, take a spoone and laye your spinage in the Frying panne euery spoonefull by him selfe, and so fry it as you woulde frye Fritters, and put it in a dish and cast sugar on it.

The VVidowes Treasure, John Partridge

Modernised recipe

- ◆ Fresh spinach
- ◆ About 6 eggs

- ◆ Handful of breadcrumbs
- ◆ Salt and sugar to taste
- ◆ Butter for frying

Boil the spinach until soft. Remove from water and allow to drain. Chop small. Put into a mixing bowl and add breadcrumbs, salt and enough eggs to create a thick batter. Allow butter to melt in the frying pan and then spoon the batter into the pan forming little individual fritters. Fry until golden brown on both sides. Serve hot and sprinkle a little sugar on top.

Additional information

The first English recipes for spinach appear in the *Forme of Cury* from 1390, where spinach is refered to as 'spinnedge or spynoches'.

Spinach became so popular that it started to replace similar leafy vegetables and herbs such as fat hen, sorrel, and orach (mountain-spinach) and it was regarded as moderately cold and moist food – ideal for hotter countries. Spinach was definitely a 'cooling' vegetable, but for cold countries such as England, it could be 'corrected' by boiling it. In 1597 botanist John Gerard says that spinach is boiled and makes people want to vomit. Young tender leaves can be used in 'sallades' and he adds, makes 'the greatest diuersitie of meates and sallades'.[17]

TO MAKE A DOUBLE FRIED MEAT OF ANY FLESH, PIGEONS OR PULLETS

Transcribed, translated original recipe

First take thy meat and make it very cleane, then cut it in quarters or in small peeces, and put it into a pan and frie it with sweet suet, stirring it with a spoone, and when it is almost boiled, take out the greatest part of the suet, then take Vergice, three or foure yolkes of egges, a little broth, and good spice, and put them into the meat, and let it boile vntill it be almost ready. Then take a little parsleyshred or beaten small and put it in a platter, and send it to the Table, sweet or sharpe according to your maisters desire.

Epulario, 1598, first booke

Modernised recipe

- ◆ 1 pullet (young chicken)
- ◆ Suet (beef fat), enough to fry the chicken pieces in
- ◆ Apple vinegar, a few spoonfuls to taste
- ◆ 3-4 egg yolks
- ◆ Spices of your choice and to taste (nutmeg, mace, ginger, cinnamon, cloves)
- ◆ Chicken stock, 1-2 cups
- ◆ Parsley, chopped fine, quantity to taste

Pre-cook the chicken in the oven until almost done. Remove, allow to cool and separate into smaller pieces. Heat the suet in a pan and fry chicken pieces until done and starting to brown. Remove from the heat, dispose of excess fat and add the stock, vinegar and spices to the pan. Allow to boil up and remove from the heat. Add egg yolks and stir in until the sauce starts to thicken a bit. Put parsley onto the serving dish, add chicken and pour sauce on top.

Additional information

Pullets, immature hens, were small – pound for pound they were more expensive than chickens and this reflected in their special status as a young, tender bird, making it something of a desirable luxury for the well-to-do. Sir Thomas Sackville favoured pullets at Christmas in 1603.[18]

Andrew Boorde suggests that they are best 'in somer, specyallye cockrellys and polettes, the whiche be vntroden'. Muffet disagrees and advises to eat them in winter. In 1603 Thomas Lodge, in his book on the plague, promoted eating pullet in times of epidemic because a humoral imbalance was thought to leave the body susceptible to plague infection and light meats such as pullet were easily digested and 'doth rectifie and temper the humors of the body'.[19]

It is interesting to note that the price for pullets was higher in London than in the country.[20]

TO BOYLE A CAPON WITH ORANGES AFTER MISTRES DUFFELDS WAY

Transcribed original recipe text

Take a Capon and boyle it with Veale or with a mary bone, or what your fancie is. Then take a good quantitie of that broth, and put it in an earthern pot by it selfe, and put thereto a good handful of Corrans, and as manie Prunes, and a few whole Maces, and some Marie, and put to this broth a good quantitie of white wine or a Claret, and so let them seeth softly together: Then take your Orenges, and with a knife scrape of all the filthinesse of the outside of them. Then cut them in the middest, and wring out the joyse of three or foure of them, put the joyse into your broth with the rest of your stuffe, then slice your Orenges thinne, and have upon the fire readie a skillet of faire seething water, and put your sliced Orenges into the water, and when that water is bitter, have more readie, and so change them still as long as you can finde the great bitternesse in the water, which will be sixe or seven times, or more, if you find need: then take them from the water, and let that runne cleane from them: then put close Oranges into your potte with your broth, and so let them stew together till your Capon be readie. Then make your sops with this broth, and cast on a little Sinamon, Ginger, and Sugar, and upon this lay your Capon, and some of your Orenges upon it, and some of your Marie, and towarde the end of the boyling of your broth, put a little Vergious, if you think best.

The Good Huswifes Handmaide for the Kitchin, 1594

Modernised recipe

- ◆ Chicken fillets
- ◆ Chicken stock (made with bone marrow)
- ◆ Handful of currants and a handful of chopped prunes
- ◆ A few blades of mace
- ◆ Cup of white wine
- ◆ 3-4 oranges (Seville oranges are best)
- ◆ 1 slice of toasted bread per person
- ◆ A sprinkle of cinnamon, ground ginger and a little sugar

Bring a pot with the chicken stock to the boil. Add chicken, currants, prunes, mace, bone marrow (optional) and wine and let it cook for about 30 minutes. In the meantime, halve the oranges and juice them. Cut the orange halves into slices and boil these in a separate pot for a few minutes. Drain the oranges, fill up with fresh water and boil again. Repeat this process until the water no longer tastes bitter. This may take up to seven times, possibly longer if you are using authentic Seville oranges. Once this is achieved, remove orange peel from the water and allow to drain. Add the orange juice to the chicken and allow to boil at medium heat for a little longer. Toast slices of bread and put onto your serving dish. Sprinkle with cinnamon, ginger and a little sugar (for good measure) and arrange chicken on top. Pour liquid on top and then decorate with your orange peel. Serve hot.

The recipe points out that you may want to add some vinegar towards the end of the cooking process if you feel it needs it.

Additional information

Capons are cockerels that have been castrated or neutered at a young age to improve the quality of their flesh for consumption. This procedure has been illegal in the UK since 1982.

In 1587 William Harrison states 'the gelding of cocks, whereby capons are made, is an ancient practice brought in of old time by the Romans when they dwelt here in this land'.[21]

Capons enjoyed a highly regarded status in the world of food for the wealthy. For their feast dinner on the first Monday in August 1564, the London Draper's Company enjoyed boiled and roast capon.[22] On 26 April 1538 a Tom Cook was paid 12s 10d for bringing capons for Thomas Cromwell.[23]

Capon was also a significant gift-food. Dyrick's wife of Greenwich was rewarded 6s 8d for bringing a capon to the palace.[24] Capons were also accepted as a means to pay rent as documents held at The Norfolk Record Office show.

Andrew Boorde was a big fan of capons. In his opinion, 'of all tame fowle a capon is moste beste'. Muffet recommends them roasted for 'moist stomacks', and boiled with sweet bone marrow in white broth to achieve an even more wholesome dish. Cogan also praises the capon above all other fowl and adds that the flesh will be more tender if the capon is killed a day or two before being eaten. Henry Butts agrees with all the others and adds that capon is healthy to eat at any time, age or constitution.[25]

The bitter 'Seville' orange is the kind of orange the wealthy Tudors were familiar with. In England the sweet Chinese orange arrived later but precisely

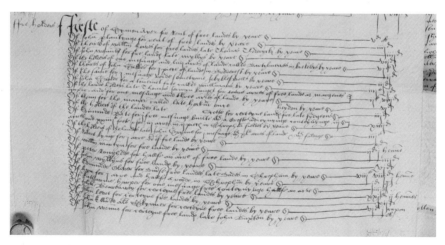

Bradcar Hall Manor Schedule, 1573. NRO, NCR 25a/24/112b. (With kind permission by Norfolk Record Office)

when is uncertain. Oranges were only used as a condiment and medicinal agent and not as an eating fruit. It is, however, likely that the Portuguese had introduced a new and better tasting variety of orange which became known as the 'Portingall' or Portugal orange. The name of the colour orange started to appear during the sixteenth century. Before then, it was simply known as 'yellow-red'.[26]

Oranges had to be mostly imported throughout Tudor England and a very few rich people had orange trees in their sheltered gardens. William Harrison describes the orange as a strange fruit that noblemen grow in their orchard.[27] In 1562 Lord Burleigh owned a rare, single orange tree, and the same year Sir Francis Carew brought a few from France which he trained against a wall sheltered with boards and stoves in winter. Sir Walter Raleigh planted orange seeds in Surrey and by 1595 he began to regularly harvest fruit.[28]

TO BOYLE CHIKINS WITH HEARBS

Transcribed original recipe

Take your Chickins and scalde them and trusse the wings on, & put their feete under the wings of your Chickins, and set them on in a little pot and scum them faire, when they have boyled: put in Spinage or Letuice and a good deale, and Rosemary, sweet butter, vergious, salt and a little Sugar and strained Bread, with a litle wine, and cut sippets, and serve it out.

A Book of Cookrye, 1591, by A.W

Modernised recipe

- One whole chicken (bound close with twine – tucking feet under wings) or individual portions to your liking
- A handful of each: fresh spinach and rosemary twigs (chopped if you prefer)
- Unsalted butter, to your liking
- A few spoonfuls of mild apple vinegar, to your liking
- Small cup of white wine
- Salt & sugar to taste
- Breadcrumbs to thicken the pottage, to your liking
- A slice of toasted bread per person, cut into strips

Boil enough water to cover your chicken in the pot. I added the rosemary at this stage to give the liquid more flavour. Cook until done. Remove the rosemary and any scum from the surface. Add spinach and the remaining ingredients. Heat up again if necessary. Put the toasted bread at the bottom of each serving bowl and scoop chicken pieces and spinach mixture on top.

Additional information

Chicken was universally praised by the Tudors as one of the healthiest foods for people of all complexions, ages and regions. It was one of the most versatile of foods in Tudor England and there were many ways on how to prepare it according to seasons and class. Domestic poultry was the most common bird of rich and poor and valued not just for their meat but also the eggs.

Unlike other animals, chickens were always the responsibility of the womenfolk. Chicken represented relatively inexpensive food and was also sold by women. Chicken was nevertheless popular at feasts and for special occasions and is frequently represented in menus for Christmas. Interestingly, the cost of purchasing it increased significantly in the second week in December and dropped again in mid-January.[29]

Live chickens were often purchased or presented as gifts and killed just before needed. On 4 July 1532 7s 6d was rewarded to a member of the public who brought 'chekons to the king grace to waltham'.[30] Thomas Cromwell's personal accounts from 1539 show a payment of 12s 3d for chickens bought by Thomas Cooke.[31]

Chickens were enjoyed across society and can be found in many purchase registers, such as the one of Thetford Priory from 1524/5 where 1£ 14s 2d was spent on various poultry and 'checons'.[32] Chicken also graced the table of Robert Dudley as his disbursement book from 20 March 1585 shows: 6s 8d was rewarded to 'Mondaies wief for presenting chickens'[33]

TO BAKE CHICKENS IN SUMMER

Transcribed original recipe

Cut off their feete, trusse them in the Coffins. Then take for everie Chicken a good handful of Gooseberies, and put into the pie with the Chickens. Then take a good quantitie of Butter, and put about everie Chicken in the pie. Then take a good quantitie of Synamon and Ginger, and put it in the pie with salt and let them bake an houre, when they bee baken, take for everie pie a yolke of an Egge, and halfe a goblet ful of Vergious, and a good quantitie of sugar, and put them all together into the pie to the Chickens, and so serve them.

The Good Huswifes Handmaide for the Kitchin, 1594, anonymous

Modernised recipe

- Fresh chicken breasts
- A handful of fresh gooseberries, cleaned and the ends snapped off
- Pastry for the pie, homemade or ready bought
- 1-2 spoonfuls of butter
- Ground cinnamon and ginger to taste
- Salt to taste
- 1 egg yolk mixed with a little mild apple vinegar and a spoonful of sugar

Parboil your chicken to play it safe and avoid salmonella. Line your pie dish with your pastry after greasing it. Place the cooked chicken, together with the gooseberries, the butter, cinnamon, ginger and the salt in your pie and close it with a pastry lid. Leave a small hole in the centre for access later. Cook for about one hour or until done at medium heat. Remove from the oven and pour vinegar/egg yolk/sugar mixture into the hole in the centre and leave to stand for a few minutes before serving.

Additional information

Similar recipes sometimes use grapes or barberries in place of gooseberries. Andrew Boorde reckons that a chicken in summer, especially a cockerel or a young hen, is nutritious. Cogan adds that there is no lighter flesh for digestion than chicken and it is agreeable to all natures, in sickness and health. Thomas Muffet explains that white chickens are thought to be the hardest to digest because they are the 'coldest and moistest of complexion' and best in summer. The flesh is best from cockerels before they crow loud and hens before the cock 'offereth to tread them'.

TO STEW A CAPON IN LEMMONS

Transcribed original recipe text

Take and slice your Lemmons, put them in a platter, and put to them white wine, Rosewater, and Sugar, and so boyle them and sugar till they be tender. Then take the best of the broth wherein your Capon is boyled: and put thereto whole mace, whole Pepper, and red Corrans, Barberies, a little Time and a good store of Marrowe. Let them boyle well together, till the broth bee almost boyled away, that you have no more than will wet your soppes. Then pour your Lemmons upon your Capon, and season your broth with Vergious and Sugar, and put it also upon your Capon.

The Good Huswifes Handmaide for the Kitchin, 1594, anonymous

Modernised recipe

- ◆ 1-2 lemons, sliced
- ◆ Cup of white wine
- ◆ A few drops of rosewater (very strong) – use sparingly!
- ◆ A few spoons of sugar to taste
- ◆ Enough chicken stock in which to boil your chicken
- ◆ Chicken fillets
- ◆ Mace blades, pepper corns, currants, dried barberries, chopped thyme to taste
- ◆ Bone marrow or a spoon of suet (beef fat)
- ◆ Apple vinegar to taste
- ◆ A few slices of toasted bread

Cook your chicken in the stock with all the other ingredients except for the lemons until most of the fluid has evaporated. Place toasted bread slices on your serving dish. Then add the chicken and the lemons. Pour the remaining fluid over the chicken and sprinkle with a little sugar and a few drops of apple vinegar.

Additional information

Lemons were first introduced to Europe via Sicily and Spain from the ninth century by Islamic armies. Crusaders had also brought back citrus fruits from the East but even by the sixteenth century, they still had to be imported and shipped to England for those with deep pockets. At a banquet given for Henry VIII and Anne Boleyn in 1533 at Westminster Hall, six silver pennies were spent on a single lemon.[34]

Before the sixteenth century, lemons were mostly used as an ingredient in poultry and meat dishes. The purchase of lemons features regularly in the *Dinner Book of the London Draper's Company*. For the period from 1563-4, 13d were spent on oranges and 4d on lemons.[35]

Essex vicar William Harrison claims in his *The Description of England* in 1587 that he has seen lemons and other strange trees brought from afar grow in noblemen's orchards.[36]

Thomas Muffet calls for temperate 'sawces' made from the juice of oranges or lemons with wine, salt and sugar for temperate meats such as capons and chickens. He explains that the pulp is cold and dry in the third degree, the peel hot and dry in the second and that lemons from Naples and Genoa are best used in sauce with flesh or fish. Englishmen living in a somewhat cooler climate to those cities are well advised to cook lemons and add wine, sugar and cinnamon to act as a form of correction.

Henry Butts advises to use lemon moderately and seldomly without the peel and conserved in sugar. In his opinion lemon is only to be used in hot weather for the youth and totally unsuited for the elderly.

TO FRIE CHICKINS

Transcribed original recipe

> Take your chickins and let them boyle in verye good sweete broath a prittye while, and take the chickens out, and quarter them out in peeces, and then put them into a frying pan with sweete butter, and let them stewe in the pan, but you must not let them be browne with frying, and then put out the butter out of the pan, and then take a little sweete broath, and as much Vergice, and the yolkes of two Egges and beate them together, and put in a little Nutmegges, synamon and Ginger, and Pepper into the sauce, and then put them all into the pan to the chickens, and stirre them together in the pan, and put them into a dish, and serue them vp.

The Good Husvvifes Jewell, 1596, Thomas Dawson

Modernised recipe

- ◆ Pieces of chicken (breasts, legs)
- ◆ Chicken stock for cooking the pieces in
- ◆ Butter for frying
- ◆ A few spoonfuls of mild apple vinegar
- ◆ 2 egg yolks
- ◆ Ground nutmeg, cinnamon, ginger and pepper to taste

Cook your chicken pieces in the broth (stock) until done. Remove and allow to drain. Melt your butter in a pan and when hot fry the chicken pieces evenly on all sides until golden. Mix the egg yolks, spices and the verjuice (vergice – apple vinegar) together. Remove excess butter from the frying pan and add the spiced vinegar-egg mixture. Stir until the egg sets and serve the sauce hot with the chicken.

Additional information

This dish is 'double' cooked: boiled and fried, a kind of remnant from earlier times. For frying meat or fish, butter, lard (pig's fat) or suet (beef fat) was used in England but only the more affluent could afford to use imported olive oil for fish days and in Lent.

Sir Elyot claimed that the meat of hens in summer nourishes little.

A PUDDING IN A COWCUMBER

Transcribed original recipe

> Liver of Lamb or Pigge, and Grapes or Gooceberries, and grated bread, pepper, salt, Cloves and mace, and a little suet, and the yolkes of three Egs, and mingle altogether and put in the Cowcumber, and let your broth boile or ever you put it in: the broth must be made of Mutton broth, Vinagre, and Butter, strained bread, and Salt, and so serve it out.

A Book of Cookrye, 1591, A.W

Modernised recipe

- 1 big cucumber
- Approx. 250g liver (lamb or pork) finely chopped or minced meat as an alternative
- Handful of fresh grapes or gooseberries
- Handful of breadcrumbs
- Pepper, salt, ground cloves & mace to taste
- A spoonful of suet
- Yolks of 3 eggs
- Lamb broth, enough to almost cover the cucumber
- A little vinegar, to taste
- A spoonful of butter
- Another spoonful of breadcrumbs

Peel and cut your cucumber in half. With a soon remove all seeds. Place your cucumber halves in an ovenproof dish. Mix the meat, grapes (or gooseberries), one spoonful of breadcrumbs, pepper, salt, cloves and mace with the suet, the egg yolks. Put this mixture inside your cucumber halves. Take your lamb broth (stock) and add the vinegar and melted butter. Pour into your ovenproof vessel very carefully – filling it up to just reach the top of the cucumbers. Transfer the dish into the oven and cook at medium heat until the meat and the cucumber are done: 5 minutes before ready, sprinkle some breadcrumbs over the cucumber and allow to brown in the oven. Serve hot.

Additional information

Cucumbers were mostly used in salads or cooked in a pottage so this recipe is rare and unusual.

Cucumber has been used in English cookery at least since the tenth century.

In 1548 Turner states that it grows in some gardens in England and has hot humoral properties.[37] Sixteenth-century garden author Thomas Hill regarded them as an enemy to lust and claimed that a thunderstorm would cause the cucumber to bend.[38]

Thomas Tusser suggests cucumbers for salads and sauces in his *Five Hundred Points of Good Husbandry* from 1577.[39]

William Harrison, the Elizabethan vicar in Essex, shares with his readers the fairly new trend of vegetables such as cucumbers being served as 'dainty dishes at the tables of delicate merchants, gentlemen and the nobility'.[40]

Cucumbers are also listed in the accounts of the London Draper's Company for the period 1570-1 and show that the Steward was paid 4d for cucumbers and oil.[41]

Physicians in Tudor England had a kind of strained relationship with this cold and wet vegetable.

Thomas Muffet advises to eat them as a salad with vinegar, salt, oil and pepper and even better, boiled with white wine, vervain (herb), dill and salt, and says they are not of 'bad nourishment', which in Tudor speak means good to eat.

In his publication of *The Haven of Health*, Thomas Cogan states that cucumbers are peeled and cut into thin slices and then served to the table with vinegar and pepper in the summer season, often together with mutton.

TO MAKE CONSERUE OF ROSES, OR OTHER FLOWERS

Transcribed original recipe

> Take the Buddes of Red Roses, somewhat before they be ready to spred: cut the red part of the leaues from ye white, then take the red leuues and beat and grind them in a stone morter with a pestell of wood, and to euery ounce of Roses, put .iii. ounces of suger in ye grinding (after the leues ar wel beaten) and grinde them together till they be perfectlye incorporated, the put it in a

glas made for the nonce: and of purpose: or els into an earthe pot: stop close, and so kepe it. Thus ye may make conserues of all kynde of flowres vsed thereunto.

The Treasurie of Commodious Conceits and Hidden Secrets, 1573, John Partridge

Modernised recipe

- ◆ A jug full of fresh, untreated rose petals (red works best)
- ◆ Caster sugar, three times the weight of petals

Cut off the white end (centre) of each petal as these are very bitter in taste. Then chop your petals as small as you can. Mix them with the sugar and fill into a jam jar allowing plenty of space to mix the mixture. Close the lid and leave the jar standing in the sun. Mix every day until the juice of the petals has been absorbed by the sugar and it is beginning to look like a jam. This process can take days, sometimes weeks, but the end result is worth it!

Additional information

To the Tudors, every food had a 'vertue', a kind of goodness to help the human body stay healthy. The virtue of this conserue of roses, according to the author of the original recipe is as such: 'Conserue of Roses comforteth the stomack, the heart and all the bowels, it molyfyeth and softneth the bowels, and is good against blacke Color: melancholy, conserues of white roses doth loose the belly more then the red.'[42]

In Tudor England there was no true red rose but only the *Rosa Gallica*, a deep pink one. Andrew Boorde, a physician in the times of Henry VIII, recommended roses for a healthy heart and brain. In 1584 Cogan informs us that the rose is cold and dry in its make-up but the red rose (*Gallica*) is less so than the white one (*Alba*). He recommends rose conserve for the use of students to comforts their head, heart and stomach.

TARTES OF RED CHERRIES

Translated, transcribed recipe

Take the reddest cherries that may be got. Take out the stones and stamp them in a mortar. Then take red roses chopped with a

knife, with a little new cheese and some old cheese well stamped with cinnamon, ginger, pepper and sugar, and all this mixed together. Add thereunto some eggs according to the quantity you will make, and with a crust of pastry bake in a pan. Being baked, strew it with sugar and rosewater.

Epulario, 1598 English translation from 1516 original Italian source

Modernised recipe

- ◆ Enough cherries for one tart (approx. 500g), destoned
- ◆ Handful of fresh, untreated rose petals, chopped finely and white heart section removed
- ◆ Cream cheese, approx. 100g
- ◆ Parmesan cheese or similar, approx. 50g or to taste
- ◆ Ground cinnamon, ginger, pepper and sugar to taste
- ◆ Eggs, 1-2 depending on amount of other ingredients

◆ Rosewater, a few drops to taste (careful – very strong in flavour)
◆ Pastry crust – homemade or ready bought for tart case

Make a tart case from fresh or use a ready-made one. Chop cherries and roses very small and mix with cheese, spices and eggs. Fill pastry cases with mixture and bake at medium heat until done. Remove from oven and sprinkle on some sugar and a few drops of rosewater on top. Serve hot or cold.

Additional information

In Tudor England cherries were generally consumed cooked but the sweet type were also eaten fresh from the tree as we can gather by Sir Thomas Elyot's observation from his book *The Castel of Helth*: 'Cheries, yf they be sweete, they do soone slyp downe into the stomake, but yf they be sowre or sharpe, they be more holsom, & do louse, yf they be eatē freshe, & newly gathered, they be cold & moyst in the first degree.' Muffet advises that all cherries are moderately cool and sweet, and ripe cherries should be preferred. Sour cherries should only be baked or made into tarts, preserved with sugar or dried after the German manner. Thomas Cogan states that cherries are cold and moist in the first degree and fresh, newly gathered cherries need eating at the beginning of dinner and not, as is the English custom, after dinner.

TO MAKE POTTAGE OF CHERRIES

Transcribed original recipe

> Fry white bread in butter til it be brown and so put it into dish, then take Cherries and take out the stones and frye them where you fried the bread then put thereto Sugar, Ginger, and Sinamon, for lacke of both, take White or Claret Wine, boyle these together, and that doon, serve them upon your Tostes.

A Booke of Cookrye, 1591, by A.W

Modernised recipe

◆ A handful of fresh cherries per person, destoned
◆ Slice of white bread, per person

- ◆ Sugar, ground cinnamon and ginger to taste
- ◆ A little white wine
- ◆ Some butter for frying

Fry your slices of bread on both sides with the butter and transfer to serving plate when golden brown. Fry the cherries in the same pan until soft. Add the spices and a little white wine if you would like the pottage to be a little juicier. Remove from the heat and serve on top of the fried bread. Enjoy hot.

This pottage makes for a tasty breakfast or served at a dessert.

Additional information

Henry Butts advises eating cherries in hot weather but in moderation to avoid 'corruption' of the body.

Cherries were purchased for the Master of the Company of Skinners' annual gathering held in June 1560. The *Dinner Book of the London Draper's Company* reveals that for their feast dinner on the first Monday in August 1565, 5lb of cherries were bought for 15d.[43]

Cherries were even good enough to entertain royalty. An observer of the festivities laid on by the Earl of Leicester for Elizabeth I when she visited Kenilworth Castle in 1575 wrote of his delight to be able to taste delicious cherries straight from their stalks. Cherries clearly made a desirable food gift and Thomas Cromwell's personal accounts from 1537 show a reward of 2s paid to William Gonson's servant for bringing cherries on 16 March.[44] Robert Dudley's account by William Chancy from 1558/9 show 12d paid to John for bringing 'cherys'.[45] Henry VIII was the lucky recipient of many presents of cherries as shown by an entry from July 1530, where the keeper of the garden in York Place was given 4s and 8d for bringing cherries to 'hamptoncourte'.[46]

TO MAKE A TARTE OF GOSEBERIES

Transcribed original recipe

> Take goseberies and parboyle them in whyte wyne, claret or ale, and boyle with all a little whyte breade, then take them up, and drawe them through a strayner as thycke as you can with the yolckes of syxe egges, then season it up with suger, halfe a dische of butter, so bake it.

A Proper Newe Booke of Cokerye, 1545/57, anonymous

Modernised recipe

- A jug full of fresh gooseberries, top and tailed
- A cup full of white wine
- A slice of white bread
- About 5 egg yolks
- Sugar to taste
- A spoonful of butter,
- A pastry case for the tart, homemade or ready bought

Bring the wine to the boil and add gooseberries and the bread. Cook until almost soft and strain the mixture through a sieve into a mixing bowl (or use a food blender). Add the egg yolks, sugar and butter. Pour this mixture into your blind baked tart case and cook at low heat until done. Serve hot or cold.

Additional information

By the 1500s gooseberries were commonly grown in England and their culinary use varied much more than we are accustomed today. Gooseberries were mostly used in tarts, sauces, and to serve as a contrast and complement to fatty meat or oily fish. They were used fermented for wine and John Gerard noted in his 'Herball' of 1597 that the young and tender leaves are eaten raw in a salad.[47] Interestingly, gooseberries do not seem to appear as food presents and that might be because they were easily available and nothing special, yet many recipes call for them.

Thomas Muffet, physician, thought thoroughly ripe gooseberries as nourishing and light, best eaten before dinner. Sweet gooseberries, in his judgement, are well suited for baking in tarts but sour ones are better served in sauce. The red gooseberries, he says, are commonly known as 'Ribes of

Apothecaries' and are colder and drier than the green variety. These are best eaten in a conserve with lots of sugar as they never grow sweet in England.

TARTE OF STRAWBERIES

Transcribed original recipe

> Seson your Strawberyes with sugar, a very little Sinamon, a little ginger, and so cover them with a cover, and you must lay upon the cover a morsel of sweet Butter, Rosewater and Sugar, you may Ice the cover if you will, you must make your Ice with the white of an egge beaten, and Rosewater and sugar.

A Booke of Cookrye, 1591, by A.W.

Modernised recipe

- ◆ Fresh strawberries, approx. 500g
- ◆ Sugar, ground cinnamon and ginger to taste

- ◆ Butter, a spoonful
- ◆ Rosewater, a few drops
- ◆ 1 egg white, beaten
- ◆ Tart case, homemade or ready bought
- ◆ Some pastry to act as a lid (homemade or ready-made)

Wash and halve your strawberries. Lay them out on your blind-baked tart bottom. Sprinkle with sugar, cinnamon and ginger. Add the butter on top. Close with a pastry lid. Mix the beaten egg white with the rosewater, sugar and spread it over the lid. Cook in the oven until the pastry is done but check on the temperature as the 'icing' tends to burn easily if the temperature is too hot. Serve hot.

Additional information

The strawberries that were available in Tudor England were more like the alpine strawberries we know today and a far cry from the big juicy ones that we are familiar with.

Strawberries were one of the few fruits the Tudors were willing to take the risk with and eat them raw, despite serious health warnings. Strawberries evoked temptation and this is very vividly portrayed in Hieronymus Bosch's *Garden of Earthly Delights* (1505) in which he used strawberries as a symbol of fleeting and dangerous pleasures.

In *The Names of Herbes* by William Turner in 1548 the entry for strawberries just states that 'every man knows well enough where they grow'.[48]

TO MAKE CONSERUE OF STRAWBERRIES (NO 51)

Transcribed original recipe

First seeth them in water, and then cast away the water, and straine them, then boyle them in white wine, and worke as before in damsons, or else straine them being ripe, then boyle them in wine and sugar till they be stiffe.

Delights for Ladies, 1602, Hugh Plat

Modernised recipe

- ◆ Fresh strawberries, washed
- ◆ Same weight in sugar
- ◆ White wine (enough to cover strawberries)

Put the strawberries in a pot and just cover with water. Allow to boil up. Remove from heat and drain water away. Return strawberries to the pot and cover with wine. Bring to the boil, remove from heat and strain through a sieve or use a food blender. Return to the pot and add the sugar. Stir and keep stirring until all the sugar has dissolved. Test every few minutes, whether the sugar has started to gel by putting a drop of the mixture onto a cold plate. If it starts to gel within a few minutes, the mixture is ready to be removed from the heat and filled into jam or earthenware pots. If the sugar test fails to gel, keep on stirring and allow the mixture to gently boil until it does. Please be aware that this mixture does burn easily if you don't stir it!

Additional information

According to Thomas Muffet's entry on strawberries in his *Health Improvements*, Melchior Duke of Brunswick was recorded to have burst asunder after having eaten too many strawberries; scary information which comes even with notes for reference! The rest of his information is more useful to us. Strawberries came in three colours: white, red and green. He considered strawberries to be agreeable in the summer – especially being eaten raw with wine and sugar or baked into a tart stuff.

Thomas Cogan informs us about the strawberries' humors: cold in first degree and dry in the second. He states that the leaves are used for medicinal purposes and the fruit is used to be eaten – made in a 'conserva like manner'.

In 1599 Henry Butts mentions that strawberries grow in the gardens as well as the woods, a firm confirmation that they were being cultivated by this time. He advises his readers to consume strawberries with wine and lots of sugar to 'correct' the ill effects of eating them.

TO MAKE GELLY OF STRAWBERRIES, MULLBERIES, RASPISBERIES, OR ANY SUCH TENDER FRUITE

Transcribed, original text

Take your beries and grinde them in an Alablaster mortar with foure ounces of sugar and a quarter of a pinte of faire water, and as much Rosewater, and so boile it in a posnet with a little peece of Isinglas, and so let it run through a fine cloth into your boxes, and so you may keepe it all the yeare.

Delights for Ladies, 1602, Hugh Plat

Modernised recipe

- ◆ Approx. 450g fresh strawberries
- ◆ Approx. 150ml fresh water with some drops of rosewater added (careful – it's strong stuff!)
- ◆ Sugar to taste, start with 100g
- ◆ 8 leaves of gelatine (substitute for Isinglas) – soaked in some of the rosewater mix

Wash and clean the strawberries. Blend with a food blender and add the sugar and the remaining rosewater mix. Transfer this mixture to a pot and bring to the boil. Add the pre-soaked gelatine and stir constantly over a LOW heat until fully dissolved. Do not allow to boil as this might prevent the gelatine from setting. Remove from the heat and pour into serving dishes or into jars and allow to set in a cool place.

Additional information

Isinglass is obtained from the dried swim bladders of fish and is one substance that the Tudors used for making gelatine.

Jellies, in particular fruit-based ones, became very popular in Elizabethan England. For their 'first quarter dinner' on 5 February 1565, the members of the London Drapers' Company had ordered forty-two jelly dishes for the ladies' table in the parlour and twenty-six for the high table in the hall at the feast dinner on 29 July 1566.[49]

Strawberries were clearly a popular choice, even with all those health warnings. They frequently feature in account books as both purchases and gifts received. In June 1560 the Master of the Company Skinners' annual meeting offered strawberries amongst all the food offered.[50]

On 8 June 1584 a gentlewoman's man of the house was rewarded 10s for bringing 'strabres' for Robert Dudley.[51] Strawberries were also a food gift fit for the king. In May 1530 Jasper the gardener at 'Beaulie' was rewarded 6s 8d for bringing 'streberyes to the king'.[52]

Food bribes were a common feature in Tudor England and the expenses of the Judges of Assize Riding the Western and Oxford circuits show, that 'extra' money bribes bought strawberries on 13 July 1598.[53]

TO BAKE PEACHES

Transcribed original recipe

Take Peaches, pare them, and cut them in tow pieces, & take out the stones as cleane as you can for breaching of the Peach: then make your pie three square to bake fowre in a pie, let your paste be verie fine, then make your dredge with fine sugar, Synamon and Ginger: and first lay a little dredge in the bottome of your pies: Then put in Peaches, and fill vp your coffins with your dredge, and put into euery coffin three spoonfuls of Rosewater. Let not your Ouen be too hot.

The Good Huswifes Handmaide for the Kitchin, 1594, anonymous

Modernised recipe

- ◆ A pastry case, homemade or ready bought
- ◆ 3-4 fresh peaches, peeled and cut in halves
- ◆ Sugar, approx. 1 cup
- ◆ Ground cinnamon and ginger to taste
- ◆ Rosewater, a few drops to taste

Blind-bake your homemade pastry case. Mix the sugar with the spices and sprinkle most of it evenly across the pastry case. Lay your Peach halves on top. Add the rest of the sugar mix on top of the peaches and a few drops of rosewater. Bake in the oven at medium heat until the peaches are soft, but the crust has not burnt.

Additional information

In the sixteenth century peaches were more commonly grown in the gardens of the wealthy and they get their first mention in the earliest printed herbal, the *Grete Herball*, published in in England in 1526 by Peter Treueris.

It is likely, that the first peach trees for cultivation reached England before the thirteenth century but improved varieties were imported during the reign of Henry VIII. Reference to this can be found in William Harrisons's publication *The Description of England* (1587) where he states that this tree can now be found in noblemen's orchards.[54]

By 1597 John Gerard can expand the list with the *avant* or *d'aunt* and the yellow peach. He describes the peach's humoral qualities as cold and moist of the second degree. They should be eaten before dinner to avoid 'putrifying other meats'.[55]

TO MAKE DRIE MARMELET OF PECHES

Transcribed original recipe

Take your Peaches and pare them, and cut them from the stones, and mince them very sinely, and steepe them in rosewater, then straine them with rosewater through a course cloth or Strainer into your Pan that you will seeth it in, you must haue to euery pound of peches halfe a pound of suger finely beaten, and put it into your pan you do boile it in; you must reserue out a good

quātity to mould your cakes or prints wihall, of that Suger, then set your pan on the fire, and stir it fil it be thick or strife that your stick wil stand vpright in it of itself, then take it vp and lay it in a platter or charger in pretty lumps as big as you wil haue ye mould or printes, and when it is colde print it on a faire boord with suger, and print them on a mould or what knot or fashion you will, & bake in an earthen pot or pan vpon ye embers or in a feate couer, and keep them continually by the fire to keep them dry.

The Second Part of the Good Hus-wiues Jewell, 1597, Thomas Dawson

Modernised recipe

- ◆ 1lb of peaches, peeled, stone removed and very finely chopped
- ◆ ½lb of jam sugar
- ◆ A few drops of rosewater in approx. 100ml water

Cook the peaches in the water with the rosewater drops for a few minutes until soft. Strain mixture through a sieve or use hand blender. Return to the pot to the heat and stir in the sugar. Allow to cook on medium heat until the mixture turns very thick – the thicker, the better. The ideal consistency is reached when a toothpick put into the mixture remains standing upright. It is very important, that you constantly stir this mixture, as it will burn as soon as you stop.

Once that stage has been reached, remove pot from the heat and spoon out the mixture into little 'lumps' on a plate to cool. The Tudors would then have often applied patterned moulds or stamps, but I have just cut mine into diamonds. These shapes can then be transferred onto a baking sheet and be dried in a warm, but not hot oven or simply kept near a radiator until dry enough to be picked up with your fingers and not feeling sticky anymore. Be warned, this can take days, sometimes weeks, depending on your mixture and humidity of your home. I made mine in October and they were just about ready for Christmas! Patience is needed for this recipe, but if you persist it makes one fine and delicious Christmas present for an utterly devoted Tudor fan!

Additional information

Galen's humoral evaluation system for the wholesomeness of food rates peaches low. Peaches were seen as liable to putrefy before being thoroughly concocted, particularly if eaten after dinner. However, condemned on the health part, they still enjoyed an elevated position amongst all the fruit – a little bit like chocolate today really.

Thomas Elyot (1490-1545) explains that peaches are cold in first degree and moist in second. Thomas Cogan explains that peaches should be eaten before a meal because as a dessert, they 'swim above' and that would corrupt all the food consumed already. He adds that ripe peaches are wholesome.

By 1599 Henry Butts is less critical and praises the peach for its pleasant taste and the ability to improve the evil, sour breath arising from the stomach, but he cannot resist the recommendation of drinking a cup of the best, most fragrant and well aromatized wine after eating peaches.

Peaches must have been quite exclusive in Tudor England as records for food presents seem to only show them in royal household accounts and even there they rarely feature. I could only find one entry for Henry VIII between 1529-31, on 18 September 1532, when 4s 8d was paid for the present of peaches to the king.[56]

In 1575, Elizabeth I received a 'box of peches of Janoa' as a New Year present.[57] This is most likely a box of candied peaches, similar to Tudor marmalade, and less likely to be a box of fresh fruit as, coming from Genoa, they would not have lasted. This recipe is very much what Elizabeth would have been given.

Chapter 3

AUTUMN

Food in Autumn and Food Preservation

In 1584 Thomas Cogan puts the start of autumn in September and advises that it is recommended to eat more than in summer: more roasted meat, drink less but stronger stuff than in summer and to beware of summer fruits. Sir Thomas Elyot warns about the dangers of autumn, which puts people of all ages, in all countries and of all dispositions at risk. According to him, autumn starts on 8 August and ends on 8 November.

Having experienced 'modern' frantic food stockpiling, for fear of not having enough food at home, and returning to traditional food preservation in very recent times, has certainly made us understand the Tudors' obsession with making food last. However, modern society seems to have lost the knowledge of sensible, meaningful food preservation and stock keeping – a very basic skill that every Tudor housewife knew inside out.

People in Tudor England were dependent on the seasons and constantly at the mercy of favourable weather conditions to secure a good harvest which would feed the family through the harsh winter months. The main concern was to stock up a variety of food that would last and see a family through from November to April. This included the purchase of salt and stockfish, salted and dried meat, dried fava beans and field peas, cereals, orchard fruit such as apples and pears warden, walnuts, hazelnuts, root vegetables and brassicas. Food preservation and conservation was the single most important activity in sixteenth-century Europe because one's life simply depended on it!

For the wealthy and nobility, however, preserves allowed for seasonal variety during the less productive food seasons. For them, autumn was a busy season of producing all kinds of sugary treats like marmalades and fruit pastes from quince, apples, pears, medlar, damson, plums, bullace and service fruit. So, while the poor had to prepare for basic survival, the wealthy had fun making treats to keep them happy through the long winter evenings.

In a time before icehouses, fridges and freezers, the Tudors had several ways to make meat, fish, vegetables and fruit last longer. Drying food naturally in the sun was often used for orchard fruit such as plums, apple, pears and certain berries. Fava beans and field peas were allowed to dry naturally on the plant before being harvested. Stockfish, the cheapest, and probably the most unpopular fish was also airdried. Ships from Bristol, which had set off in February and March, returned to sell their salted and air-dried cod at the autumn markets such as Stourbridge, where people stocked up for the winter. Meat could also be airdried and was sometimes smoked at the same time; prosciutto is one example of these methods still being used in Europe today.

In Tudor England farmers tried to keep their livestock going as long as they could during the autumn. Pigs were taken into the forest to fatten up on acorns and nuts. Around Martinmas, in November, those animals destined for slaughter and needed for salted or smoked cured meat were traditionally slaughtered. However, during the sixteenth century farmers started to spread out the slaughter, as Thomas Tusser advises in his *A Hundred Good Pointes of Husbandrie* from 1557 (No31)

> At Hallowmas, slaughter time, sone commeth in:
> and then doth the husbande mans, feasting begin.
> From that time, to Candlemas, weekely kill some:
> their offal for household, the better shall come.

With the onset of winter, there was a clear predominance of salted meat over fresh. The most common way to preserve meat and fish was the use of salt, which naturally kills off any bacteria responsible for food decay. The best example of this preserving method we find in brawn, a particular Christmas staple in Tudor England. Originally made from cured meat of a wild boar's head, by the sixteenth century a domesticated pig was used instead. The precise preparation of brawn, which was left in strong brine (salt water), started months before Christmas as described by William Harrison and Thomas Muffet. Preserved meats also appear as gifts given to influential people by members of the public. On the first of July 1585 a Mrs Barates was awarded 10s for sending Robert Dudley, Earl of Leicester, preserved meat at Wanstead that day.[1]

Large quantities of beef and mutton were also laid in brine, sometimes for up to a month in winter. 'White' herring was gutted, brined for fifteen hours and packed in layers of salt barrels. 'Red' herring was brined and hung up in smoky sheds to dry out which gave them the red colour. Salt was also added to butter and cheese to prevent them from going rancid too quickly.

The most cost-effective way of preserving was pickling, which is the submersion of food in salted vinegar. Sixteenth-century recipes include mostly vegetables such as samphire, cucumbers, tree buds, capers, flowers and stalks. Towards the end of Elizabeth's reign, we also see meat and herring being preserved by this method. Sauerkraut is cabbage in brine, but also fermented and appears to be more common on the Continent than England.

Other more obscure means of preserving food that we no longer apply are the submersion of fruit in honey, the baking of meat and fish inside a pie and the use of molten butter as a 'sealant', all of which exclude airborne bacteria. Gallypots are often mentioned in sixteenth-century preserving recipes and were specially designed for conservation and the use of butter as a sealant.

In the autumn orchard fruit was picked and stored for future use. Tudor varieties of apples and pears such as the warden pear are naturally more suited to longer storage, and unlike modern pears, they do not become soft without the process of cooking. In the kitchen garden cabbages, beet (chard), leek, parsnip and turnip overwintered if they were protected from deer. Parsnip actually benefits from being 'frozen' in the ground as it stimulates the plant to increase its sugar content, making it a natural and cheap source of sugar.

Sugar was the preserving agent of choice by those who could afford it. Late-Tudor cookery books and recipe collections adopted the use of this white miracle 'spice' instantly and made full use of it – providing a wide range of recipes for preserving fruit such as cherries, strawberries, quince, warden, apple, plum, damson, gooseberries, medlar, apricot, peach, orange and lemon – ready to be consumed when the season was long over. The use of sugar in excess quickly became the means of showing off financial power and status, especially in a time when well-to-do merchants and other financially successful but untitled 'gentleman' had to prove their elevated position in high society. Hugh Plat believed that conserves signalled a triumphant human mastery of nature. The poem in the preface of his book *Delights for Ladies*, first published in 1602, opens with 'The Art of Preserving':

> When chrystall frosts hath nipt the tender grape,
> And cleane consume'd the fruits of every vine,
> Yet beere behold the clusters fresh and faire,
> Fed from the branch, or hanging on the line.
> The walnut, small nut, and the Chestnut sweete,
> Whose sugred kernels loose their pleasing taste,
> Are here from yeere to yeere preserved,
> And made by Arte with strongest fruites to last.
> Th'artichoke, the apple of such strength,
> The Quince, the Pomgranate, with the Barberie,
> No sugar us'd, yet colour, taste, and smell,
> Are here maintain'd and kept most naturally

The term 'preserve' or 'conserve' could be used for both food and humans and it meant 'maintaining life by warding off disease, keeping people energetic and eradicating the effects of age', something that still concerns us today.

Spices in Tudor recipes were not used for the preservation of food but for the preservation of the human body that was to consume the food. The intention was to stop the decay of the human body caused by bad air or bad food. Spices in the sixteenth century were not as expensive as they previously were but certain ones were still highly regarded for their flavour, medicinal benefits and to a lesser degree as a food marker for the very rich. However, it has to be stressed that the often-repeated 'fact' that spices were used to cover up rotten meat or food makes absolutely no sense and was probably made up by the Victorians to sell a good story. Spices were still a reasonably expensive commodity and would not have been wasted on poor quality meat. William Harrison in *The Description of England* allows us an insight into how much spices cost in 1587: 'nutmegs at 2½ d. the ounce, ginger at a penny the ounce, cinnamon at 4d. the ounce, cloves at 2., and pepper at 12d. and 16d the pound.'[2] For the feast dinner of the London Draper's Company in 1580, 54s 4d was spent on cinnamon, nutmeg, grains of paradise, coriander seeds, cloves, pepper, saffron, mace and ginger.[3]

Spices also made good gifts when you needed to get into somebody's good books. On 8 May 1535 John Husee sent a whole load of items to Lord Lisle to 'recommend' himself. Amongst the many goods were fine sugar loaves, 2lb of cinnamon, 2lb of ginger, 1lb of cloves, 1lb of mace, and ten 10lb of pepper.[4]

Unlike us, the Tudors were on top of their food management and to allow food to perish would be simply unacceptable in a Tudor household. Spices were kept under lock and key in a spice cupboard which contained a number of essentials such as pepper, cinnamon, ginger, nutmeg, mace, cloves, saffron, caraway, aniseed and fennel seed. Except for the last, all had to be imported from warmer climates.

Pepper came in a number of varieties including black, white, long pepper and cubeb pepper. Both long and cubeb peppers suffered a decline during the Tudor epoch and black pepper was no longer as prestigious and expensive as it had been throughout the medieval age. It was imported from India while cubebs came from Africa. All types of peppers were considered 'hot' and Andrew Boorde believes black pepper to 'make a man leane'.

Cinnamon was imported from Sri Lanka and the trade routes were closely controlled by Arabs until the sixteenth century when the Portuguese started trading with Sri Lanka and hence opened the cinnamon trade to England directly. Cassia cinnamon was the cheaper alternative but was to be avoided as excessive use may cause liver damage.

Mace is the outer skin of the nutmeg, dried into blades. In Tudor England mace was more commonly used than nutmeg. It was imported from the Moluccas islands (now Indonesia) which were known as the Spice Islands and much fought over by the Spanish, Portuguese, Dutch and English during the sixteenth century. Nutmeg was a key flavour in Elizabethan recipes, though excessive use can cause hallucinogens and induce miscarriages.

Saffron was grown in England by the Tudor period and the centres lay in Essex, Norfolk and Cornwall. The town of 'Walden' changed its name to 'Saffron Walden' in the sixteenth century and the flower still decorates many houses and is used in the town's coat of arms. According to Andrew Boorde, saffron 'doth comforte the herte & the stomacke, but he is to hote for the lyuer'.

Caraway seeds were used as a breath freshener and to aid digestion and alleviate flatulence. Aniseed was commonly used in desserts. Both caraway seeds and aniseed were imported from Egypt and Greece. Boorde recommends aniseed with the consumption of pears. Fennel seeds were most often used coated in numerous layers of sugar, known as comfits.

Potage (Pottage) in Tudor England

Pottage or potage was the basic daily dish of cooked food for mostly common folk, giving scope for indefinite variations according to the season, the locality or day, but it could be dressed up with many extras or remain simple with root vegetables, herbs and cereal. Pottage was a stew cooked in a pot, a most nourishing dish of cereals, pulses, greens and herbs with sufficient meat or fish to give it a satisfying, rich flavour.

References to food of ordinary people are sparse until after 1550 but there is a kind of early description by Juan Vives, Princess Mary's tutor and an Oxford professor, in his *Dialogues*, written before 1540. This is a collection of Latin translation exercises for his students at a school in Bruges. In one of those dialogues the students inform us that they were expected to eat moderately of the pottage made from bones, sometimes meat, cereal, rice, turnip, coleworts, peas, beans and lentils, but could have as much bread as they liked.

In the 1540s John Hales, MP and author of health advice literature, described his stereotyped picture of poor man's food as 'food sodden, pottage of some kind and bread sops with greenstuff as common fare'.

In the recipe book *A Book of Cookre* (1591) every pottage started with a broth made with a piece of beef, marrow from bones, pepper, salt, verjuice, ale (wine), and for the wealthier, dates, sugar and mace. The broth was then thickened at the last moment with egg yolks and seasoned with herbs such as endive, succory, marigolds, marjoram, parsley, thyme and rosemary.

According to cookery book author Thomas Dawson, the first move for making dinner was the preparation of a broth. This did not necessarily involve the use of onion or garlic.

Broth for fish used water, yeast, herbs, mace, prunes, verjuice, vinegar and butter.

Pottages were sold to members of the public in inns, which had a bad reputation and were known to reheat their cooked meals according to the book written in 1561 *Regimen for going on the road*. During the second half of the sixteenth century food had become worthy of literary comment, but interestingly Shakespeare does not mention pottage in any of his works.

Recipes

MEAT OF YOUNG BEANES WITH FLESH

Translated original recipe

To make meat of young Beanes with flesh or otherwise. Take Beanes and blanch them with whot water like almonds, then set them to boile, and when they are boiled, put to them a little Parsely, and Mints well beaten, and seeth them with salt Beefe or Bacon, let it be somewhat green and it is the better. The like may be done with pease and other fruits when they are greene.

English translation of *Epulario*, 1598

Modernised recipe

- ◆ Fresh or frozen fava beans (broad beans)
- ◆ Fresh or frozen parsley, mint – finely chopped
- ◆ Cubed beef or bacon (salted works best)

Boil the beans in salted water until their shells open. Drain, allow to cool and remove the shells by squeezing them. Return the shelled beans to the pot and fill up with about one litre of water. Bring to the boil and add the meat. Reduce the heat and allow to cook for at least two hours on low heat. If you use unsalted meat, add some salt. When both meat and beans are soft, add the herbs and serve hot with some fresh bread.

Additional information

The bean most frequently grown in Tudor England was the fava or broad bean and the black-eyed pea (bean) which confusingly was called *phaseolus* in Latin, the name that was given later to the new world species (*phaseolus vulgaris*) which really became commonly used only from the very late sixteenth century in England. Beans were seen as a 'gross' (heavy and coarse) foodstuff, difficult to digest and suitable for labourers only.

Beans started losing their stigma only towards the close of the sixteenth century. This was probably helped by the new way of eating fava beans fresh, immature and green rather than fully dried from the field.

Beans were one of the main staples for the majority of people in Tudor England and it was essential for surviving the long winter when the grain stock run out. Dried, they lasted easily through the winter and could be used in potage, mashed or even ground into flour and used for making bread. William Harrison described beans as 'horse corn' and goes on to say that they are being used by the labouring class in pottages and in times of hardship for making bread.[5]

POTAGE OF BEANES

Translated, original recipe

Take Beanes a little broken, make them very cleane and set them on the fire, and when the water boileth cast it away, and put more water that it may bee higher then the Beanes by two fingers, then casting in some salt, set them to séeth vpon the coals on a soft fire, couering them, and let them boile well: that done, dry them, and stampe them in a morter, then boile them againe in a pipkin with good oyle, and let them séeth well , but burne them not, then take a little sage and sigges, or apples cut small, and put it into the Oyle with Onyons, and softly them then dish them and put some of the oyle and other mixtures vpon them with good spices

English translation of *Epulario,* 1598

Modernised recipe

- ♦ Fresh or frozen fava beans (broad beans)
- ♦ A few spoonfuls of olive oil

- ◆ Fresh or frozen sage, chopped finely
- ◆ 1 small apple, peeled and chopped finely
- ◆ 1 onion, peeled and chopped finely
- ◆ Ground nutmeg, mace, pepper for decoration

Boil your beans in water until their shells start to split. Drain, allow to cool and remove shells by squeezing them. Put shelled beans back in the pot and fill up with water until they are submerged. Add salt and allow them to boil until they are very soft. Drain excess fluid and either crush them to a paste in a big mortar or use a hand blender. Add enough water until the potage reaches the texture to your liking and allow to simmer at low heat. In the meantime, lightly fry your onions and apples in some of the oil and then mix into the bean potage together with the sage. Serve with some oil drizzled on top and spices of your choice sprinkled on for decoration!

Additional information

Physicians were very suspicious about the bean's effect on the health of affluent and not physically active people. Flatulent food such as beans were thought to literally send fumes throughout the body, swelling it, or worse rising into the brain and causing nightmares. This could then further 'inflate' the extremities and genitals – the very reason why they were also often considered aphrodisiacs.[6]

Thomas Cogan regarded them as difficult to digest. Cogan explains that the 'faba' beane' is cool and dry and 'green Beans before they be ripe are cold & moyst, but when they drie they have power to binde and restrain'. He believes that they are equally well eaten green or dry: the green beans with butter and the dry beans with salt and no butter. Interestingly, he adds that in 'Leycester shire they make bread for their family – and I meane not hors-bread.'[7]

Thomas Muffet states that beans were at first grown in the fields but 'lately been set and kept in gardens'. He tells us that they are very hurtful unless eaten very young (green) and cooked in a fat broth with their husk removed.[8] They are best consumed at the beginning of a meal or in the midst of it – buttered, sprinkled with gross pepper and salt. In 1599 Henry Butts advises to eat them without their husk with salt and majoram and well cooked. He confirms that they are cold in the first and dry in the second degree and best eaten in cold weather for 'grosse and homely feeders'.

It is somehow not surprising at all that beans do not feature in the household accounts of the affluent and nobility. If they did use them they would have come directly from their gardens and therefore would not feature in any expenses. Beans do make an occasional appearance in the household accounts of merchants, gentry and priories as the one occasion when 6s 10d was paid for beans in the Norwich Cathedral Priory Gardener's accounts in 1480.[9]

TO MAKE BROTH OF A GOURD

Translated, original recipe

> Make them cleane as they ought to bee, then seeth them in flesh broth, or else with water alone, adding thereto certaine Onions as you thinke good, and when it is boiled take it out, then either bruse it small or stampe it, and straine it through a Cullander, and then againe set it to seeth in a pipkin with fat broth, and a little Veriuice, and let them bee somrwhat yellow with Saffron, and when they are sod take them off the fire, and set them to coole, then take yolkes of Egges according to the quantity, and

beat them with a little old cheese, and put them to the said meat, stirring it with a spoone least it smell of the smoke, then dish it and cast spice vpon it.

Epulario, second book, English translation 1598

Modernised recipe

- ◆ 1 gourd (peeled and chopped with seeds removed)
- ◆ 1 onion (peeled and quartered)
- ◆ Chicken or lamb stock, enough to cover gourd pieces
- ◆ Apple vinegar, to taste
- ◆ Small number of saffron strands (stamped/crushed in a mortar)
- ◆ Small number of egg yolks
- ◆ Ground hard cheese such as parmesan, to taste
- ◆ Spices of your choice such as nutmeg, mace, pepper, salt, cinnamon, ginger

Boil your gourd and onion in the meat stock until soft. Strain through a colander or use hand blender. Return to the pot, add a little more stock if required. Season with apple vinegar and saffron. Quickly allow to boil up again, remove from the heat and stir in egg yolks and ground cheese. Dish out and sprinkle some dark spice on it.

Additional information

According to John Harvey gourds have been cultivated in English gardens at least since the tenth century with Aelfric being the first to mention them in 995.

William Turner, Dean of Wells Cathedral between 1551-4 and 1560-8 mentions them in his *The Name of Herbes* (1548), and apart from confirming that they are cold and moist in the second degree, provides no more detailed information.[10] Thomas Tusser's instructions in *Five Hundred Points of Good Husbandry* (1557) advises to sow gourds in May.[11]

In 1587, William Harrison describes several vegetables – gourds being one of them – as being 'fed upon as dainty dishes at the tables of delicate merchants, gentlemen and the nobility'.[12] Herbalist John Gerard's description of a ripe gourd matches the appearance of a modern, overripe marrow. He advises to either boil the 'pulp' but even better, bake or fry the gourd to counterbalance the cold and moist nature.[13]

The gourd referred to by all these Tudor authorities is a different species to the one that was introduced from the Americas and includes squashes like butternut, and softer ones like zucchini (courgette). The origin of the 'pumpkin' is still debated – Americas or Asia, nobody can tell for sure yet and more research is needed.

Interestingly, several Tudor physicians group gourds together with 'fruits' such as cucumbers, 'pompions'(pumpkin) and melons. Andrew Boorde is clearly not a fan and calls them 'of evil nourishment'. Sir Thomas Elyott states their natural make-up as cold and moist in the second degree and observes that they are very unpleasant to eat raw. Recommended cooking methods are boiling, toasting and frying. Thomas Muffet recommends boiling, baking or frying with butter for this potentially very unwholesome food in his *Health's Improvement*. In 1599 Henry Butts advises to eat gourds with pepper, mustard, vinegar, hot herbs such as onions and parsley to make them more agreeable and correct all the humoral shortfall.

TO SOWCE A PIGGE

Transcribed original recipe

> You must take White Wine, and a litle sweet broth, and half a score of Nutmegs cut in quarters; Then take sweete Margeram, Rosemary, Baies, and Time, and let them boil all together, scum them verie cleane: and when they be boyled, put them in an earthen pan, and the syrop also: and when ye serve them, a quarter in a dish, and the Baies, and Nutmegs on the top.

The Good Husvvifes Jewell, Thomas Dawson, 1596

Modernised recipe

- Roasted pork fillet, cut into slices
- Cup of meat stock
- Cup of white wine
- 1-2 fresh or dried bay leaves
- Fresh rosemary, marjoram, thyme sprigs
- Very coarsely ground nutmeg to taste

Cook the stock, the wine, nutmeg and the herbs for about 20 minutes. Remove from the heat and skim off all herbs. I allowed the roast fillet to soak in this broth for about half an hour before serving it. As the recipe suggests, decorate it with the bay leaves and the nutmeg if you wish.

Additional information

This sauce reminds me very much of the very thin ones of a century earlier. It is pleasant in taste, easy to prepare and works well with left over roast pork.

Pork was eaten by all levels of society in sixteenth-century England and could be preserved in many ways: smoked ham, bacon, sausages, pickled or salted (brawn).

Pigs were kept solely for their meat, were economical to keep and were mostly slaughtered in the autumn. The fat from pigs, called lard, was mostly used by the lower class instead of butter.

The amount of pork consumed varied from estate to estate and depended much on preference as well as availability. The Expenses of the Judges of Assize Riding the Western and Oxford Circuits 1596-1601 shown an entry of 18d spent on a roast pig for the provision bought at Winchester in 1596.[14]

Despite pork being consumed across society, there were those who actively disliked it such as Andrew Boorde. Sir Thomas Elyot also remained on the cautious side and said that Galen recommended it. Pork, he felt, was really only good for young people and those who physically worked hard. Thomas Muffet agrees and claims that pork enjoys a much better reputation than it deserves. In his *Health's Improvement*, he admits that the taste is pleasant but calls it the 'mother of many mischiefs'. He advises those that eat pork to roast it and to fill the belly with salt, vinegar and sage as this would make it less offensive. In his opinion one must drink wine with pork and if not available, then with a good draught of the strongest beer well spiced with ginger. After the consumption it is essential to 'labour it out' as ploughmen do.

Thomas Cogan is one source who mentions that the 'flesh of a swine hath such likenesse to mans flesh, both in savor and tast, that some have eaten mans flesh in stead of porke'. In 1599, Henry Butts is less worried, and he notes that pork is good food to eat in cold weather.

The use of bay (leaves) is an interesting one as this was a relative newcomer in Elizabethan England. It is possible that the recipe is referring to bay berries as mentioned by Thomas Muffet (1553-1604) in his book *Health's Improvement*. From John Gerard's Herball (1597/1633) we learn that both the leaves and the berries were used. Both share the same humors: hot and very dry. According to him, physicians boil the leaves with meat and fish to reduce the urge to vomit.[15]

TO BAKE A PIGGE

Transcribed original recipe text

> Take your Pig and flea it, and draw out all that clean which is in his bellye, and wash him clean, and perboyle him, season it with Clove, mace, nutmegs, pepper & salt, and so lay him in the paste with good store of Butter, then set it in the Oven till it be baked inough.

A Book of Cookrye, 1591, A.W

Sauce from *The Good Hous-wiues Treasurie*, 1588: 'Porke Sauce: Take Vineger, Mustard, Suger and Pepper'.

Modernised recipe

- ◆ Pork fillet
- ◆ Pastry (ready-made or homemade)
- ◆ Ground cloves, ground nutmeg, ground pepper and salt to taste
- ◆ A few spoonfuls of unsalted butter

Grease your pie dish and dust it with flour. Line it with your pastry and leave enough to cut a lid. Pre-boil your pork fillet for about half an hour, remove from the water and slice it. Lay it into your pie dish and season with spices. Top with butter and close with the pastry lid. Bake at medium heat in the oven until done, which is around one hour.

I served this dish with a mustard and vinegar sauce and they complement each other beautifully. Pork was often served with mustard or a mustard-based sauce because it was the, physician's belief that the naturally 'cold and moist' pork should be corrected by 'hot and dry' mustard and that the mustard's natural qualities will aid the digestion of pork. The cooking process of 'dry' cooking such as roasting or baking would also have helped to 'correct' the 'wet' humors of pork.

Additional information

Pork's reputation as only suitable for physical active people was mentioned by the likes of Henry Butts, a Cambridge don who in 1599 deemed it best for those who took exercise, such as labourers and the young. However, generally pork and bacon were deemed nutritious and worthy meats for all classes and not associated as poor man's food until after the sixteenth century. Physician Thomas Muffet (1553-1604) declares that pork is 'sweet, luscious and pleasant to wantons, and earnestly desired of distempered stomachs'.[16]

Many estates reared their own pigs as they were relatively economical to feed, but if you had to buy pork, according to a royal proclamation made by Henry VIII in 1544, the price you had to pay was 3/4d for a pound.[17] Salt pork was mostly supplied to soldiers and fresh pork reached the kitchens of many grand estates.

TO MAKE VAUNTS

Transcribed original recipe

> Take marrow of Beefe, as much as you can hold in both your hands, cut it as big as a great dice. Then take ten prunes and cut the fruit from the stones, then take halfe a handful of Corrans, washe them and picke them, then put your marrow in a cleane platter, and your Dates, Prunes and Corrans, washe them and picke them, then put your marrow in a cleane platter, and your Dates, Prunes and Corrans: then take ten yolks of Egs, and put into your stuffe afore rehearsed. Then take a quartwen of Sugar, and more, and beat it small and put it to your marrow. Then take two spoonfuls of Synamon, and a spoonful of sugar, and put them to your stuffe, and mingle them all together, then take eight yolkes of Egs, and four spoonfuls of Rosewater, straine them, and put a little Sugar to it. Then take a faire frying pan, and put a little peece of butter in it, as much as a walnut, and set it upon a good fire, and when it looketh almost blacke, put it out of your pan, and as fast as you can, put halfe of the yolkes of Egs, into

the midst of your pan, and let it run all the bredth of your pan, and frie it faire and yellow, and when it is fried put it in a faire dish, and put your stuffe therein, and spread it al te bottom of the dish, and then make another vaunt even as you made the other, and set it upon a faire borde and cut it in faire slices, of the breadth of your little finger, as long as your vaunt is: then lay it upon your stuffe after the fashion of a lettice window, and then cut off the ends of them, as much as lyeth without the inward compasse of the dish. Then set the dish within the Oven or in a baking pan, and let it bake with leisure, and when it is baken ynough the mattow will come faire out of the vaunt, unto the brim of the dish. Then draw it out, and cast theron a little sugar, and so you may serve it in.

The Good Huswifes Handmaide for the Kitchin, 1594 edition, anonymous

Modernised recipe

I have halved the quantities from the original recipe and instead of beef marrow I used beef mince as I was unable to source the required amount in bone marrow.

- ◆ Handful of beef mince (full fat) instead of bone marrow
- ◆ ½ handful each of prunes, dates, currants – all finely chopped
- ◆ 5 egg yolks and 2 whole eggs
- ◆ Caster sugar to your taste (the recipe calls for a quart or two pints, which seems to be way too much, even when halved in quantity as I did)
- ◆ 1 spoonful of ground cinnamon
- ◆ A few drops of rosewater
- ◆ Butter for frying

Mix the meat, dates, currants and prunes with the sugar, rosewater drops, cinnamon and three egg yolks. Melt the butter in a pan at medium heat. Mix one egg with one extra yolk and pour into the pan. Let it set at medium heat and then remove from the pan. Take the remaining egg and yolk, mix and pour evenly into the pan. Cook at medium heat until set. Add your meat mixture evenly and allow another few minutes cooking at medium heat. Put the removed set egg mixture back on top of the now almost cooked meat layer and allow a few minutes to cook at a fairly gentle heat until all the meat has thoroughly cooked. You can carry out all these stages in the oven with an oven-proof dish if you prefer. Sprinkle with sugar before you serve.

Additional information

Vaunts are stuffed, sweet omelettes. They were made with dried fruits, spices and meat or bone marrow – all bound with egg yolks and sandwiched between two layers of cooked egg mixture. According to the Oxford English Dictionary, the term 'vaunt' was used to describe this dish, first appeared in the *Boke of Keruynge* in 1508.

Marrow from bones was considered a prized delicacy in Tudor England and often used to start a broth or even eaten as a dish in its own right. Tudor physicians believed marrow to be hot and moist in its humoral make-up. Sir Thomas Elyot claims, that it is 'yll' for the stomach but for those who can stomach it, marrow offers much nourishment.

FOR TO BAKE A GAMMON OF BACON

Transcribed original recipe

> Boyle your gammon of Bacon and stuffe it with Parsley and Sage, and yolks of hard Egs, and when it is boyled, stuffe it and let

it boyle again, season it with Pepper, Cloves, and Mace, sticke whole Cloves fast in it: Then lay it so in your paste with salte butter, and so bake it.

The Good Huswifes Handmaide for the Kitchin, 1594, anonymous

Modernised recipe

- ◆ Piece of gammon
- ◆ Shortcrust pastry, homemade or ready bought
- ◆ Fresh parsley and sage, chopped
- ◆ 2 hard boiled eggs, chopped
- ◆ Pepper, whole cloves and ground mace to taste
- ◆ Salt to taste
- ◆ A little butter to taste

Boil your meat in water until cooked. Remove and allow to drain. Roll out pastry and put gammon on top. Cut meat along the top and insert the eggs, herbs and ground spices. Stick whole cloves into the meat. Sprinkle meat with salt and put a knob of butter on top. Close up with pastry and bake at medium heat until done.

Additional information

Bacon was considered more suitable for the labouring class as Andrew Boorde clearly states in 1542: 'Bacon is good for carters and plowmen, the whiche be euer labourynge in the earth or dunge.' However, this is somehow contradictory to contemporary sources as this recipe, clearly aimed at the better-off, middle-class market of merchants, shows. There is also a mention of a gammon of bacon in the household accounts and disbursement books of Robert Dudley, Earl of Leicester, where we find an entry for 2s 6d 'gyen in reward the same day by your lordship's commandment to Mrs Note's man for presenting grene geese, a pyg and a gamon of bakon to your lordship at Croydon' on 27 April 1585.[18]

Bacon was also bought for 3s 2d for the first Quarter Dinner on 13 January 1564 as the dinner book of the London drapers' company shows.[19]

The Autumn Assizes of the judges for the first five counties, begun in Winchester Castle on 10 July 1598, were also the grateful recipients of a food gift comprising one gammon of bacon in a pie.[20]

Bacon was gripped by the carver's left thumb and two forefingers while it was cut, like venison, and it was also served on a bed of pease pottage.[21]

TO MAKE A FLORENTINE

Transcribed original recipe

> Take Veale, and some of the kidney of the loyne, or cold Veale roasted, cold capon or feasant, which of them you will, and minse it verie small, with sweet Suet, put on to it two or three yolkes of Egges, being hard soode, Corans and Dates small shred. Season it with a litle Sinamon and ginger, a very litle Cloves and Mace, with a litle salt and sugar and a litle Time finely shred. Make your paste fine with butter and yolks of egs, and sugar, rolle it very thin, and so lay it in a platter with butter underneath, and so cut your cover and lay it upon it.

The Good Huswifes Handmaide for the Kitchin, 1594, anonymous

Modernised recipe

- ◆ Minced veal, chicken, pheasant or kidney
- ◆ A little suet (beef fat)

- ◆ 2-3 egg yolks (hard boiled)
- ◆ Currants and dates, finely chopped, to taste
- ◆ Ground cinnamon, ginger, cloves and mace to taste
- ◆ Salt and sugar to taste
- ◆ Fresh or frozen thyme, chopped, to taste
- ◆ Shortcrust (homemade or ready bought) pastry
- ◆ A spoonful of butter

Butter and sprinkle flour on the bottom of you pie dish. Roll out shortcrust pastry and lay into your baking dish. Keep enough to cut a lid. Mix meat with other ingredients and spread on top of your pastry. Close it with the pastry lid. Bake it in the oven at medium heat for about 1 ½ hours or until done.

Additional information

A Florentine was a kind of pie or tart, especially with meat baked in a dish with a cover of pastry. According to the Oxford English Dictionary, the earliest known use of this term used for food dates to 1579 from E Hake's *Newes out of Powles Churchyarde newly Renued, IV. Sig*.

In 1587, William Harrison mentions *Florentines* in his *Description of England* when he describes how even merchants now have their own feasts.[22]

TO BOILE MUTTON FOR SUPPER

Transcribed original recipe

> Take Carret rootes, and cut them an inch long, take a handful of parselie and time halfe chopped, and put into the pot the Mutton, and so let them boyle, being seasoned with Salte and pepper, and so serue it foorth.

The Second Part of The Good Huswifes Iewell, 1597, Thomas Dawson

Modernised recipe

- Fresh or frozen carrots, peeled and cut into 1-in slices
- Fresh or frozen parsley and thyme, finely chopped

- ◆ Mutton or lamb
- ◆ Salt and pepper to taste

Chop the meat into bite-size chunks and boil with the carrots until soft at medium heat, covered or in an ovenproof dish if you prefer. When soft, add the salt and pepper and the herbs.

Additional information

From *The Boke of Kerynge* (1508) we know that boiled meat was generally cut into small cubes and set on a bed of their particular potage, so that the lord could eat them with his spoon.[23]

According to *A Proper New Book of Cookrye* (1545), mutton was good to eat all throughout the year. [24] Thomas Dawson shows a clear preference for mutton over beef and pork in his cookery book.

Carrots were introduced from Islamic countries in the late Middle Ages, reaching England in the fourteenth and fifteenth centuries. Through selective breeding, the size, flavour and colour improved. Most carrots in Tudor England were purple, yellowish and red. Orange became popular in the seventeenth century. All root vegetables, carrots included, were seen as cheap and substantial food. The *Dinner book of the London Draper's Company* shows that for the Quarter Dinner on 3 May 1564 4d was spent on carrots and spinach.[25]

Thomas Cogan gives carrots a hot and dry classification and adds that the carrot's virtue is that of breaking wind. He states that carrots are eaten boiled and then buttered and are the common food for the common people all through the autumn and on fish days.

Thomas Muffet praises carrots for the aromatical and spice-like taste and recommends boiling in a fatty broth or buttered. The more yellow the root, the sweeter, more tender and aromatic the carrot is.

Henry Butts, in 1599, proclaims carrots to be some kind of aphrodisiac being very windy and slowly digested. He recommends thorough boiling and then dressing in oil, mustard and coriander. In his opinion, carrots are suited best for cold weather and for all people but the elderly.

Mutton was probably the most common meat in the English diet of the sixteenth century. It was also not attached to any particular class. Mutton was generally reasonably priced and affordable to many. The gentlemen judges Thomas Walmsley and Edward Fenner, who rode the western circuit from July to Autumn 1596, gladly accepted one mutton from Mr Maior of Winton and his brethren as a gift.[26]

The Dinner book of the London Draper's Company shows that for a feast dinner in 1568 4s was paid for half a mutton 'for breakfast'.[27] Sir Thomas Elyot rates it as a temperate meat which is used more than any other. Thomas Muffet recommends mutton because it is good for all ages but best no older than four years old. The best mutton, he says, comes from Norfolk, Wiltshire and Wales.

TO MAKE GOOD GARLIKE SAUCE

Transcribed, translated recipe

> Take blanched Almonds well stamped, and being halfe beaten, put as much Garlike to them as you thinke good, and stampe them together, tempering them with water least it be oiley, then take crummes of white bread what quantity you will, and soke it either in leane broth of flesh or fish as time serueth: this sauce you may kéepe & vse with all meats, fat or leane as you thinke good.

Epulario, 1598 translation

Modernised recipe

- A handful of ground almonds
- Fresh, crushed garlic to taste
- A handful of breadcrumbs
- Approx. 500ml of meat or vegetable stock

Put all ingredients into the stock, allow to cook for a few minutes and then leave to stand for a few minutes. You can serve this sauce with any roast meat of your choice.

Additional information

This recipe is unusual as it mentions garlic, but it also points to its Italian origin.

Garlic was a popular flavouring in sixteenth-century southern Europe but in England it was mostly associated with the lower class. Scholars were generally advised to avoid foods whose fumes 'damaged the brain by smothering the intellect and understanding', garlic being one of that group.[28]

Garlic was believed to be difficult to digest, which is how they explained the bad breath it causes. Garlic was also used for good circulation of the blood.

TO MAKE A TARTE OF HIPPES

Transcribed original recipe

> Take Hippes and cutte them, and take the seedes out, and wash them verye cleane, and put them into your Tarte, and season them with suger, cinnamon and ginger. So you must preserue them with suger, Cinamon and Ginger, and put them into a gelly pot close.

The Good Husvvifes Jewell, 1596, Thomas Dawson

Modernised recipe

- Organic rosehips, cut in half and all seeds removed
- Same amount in sugar
- Cinnamon and ginger to taste

Boil the rosehips in just enough water so they remain covered. When they are soft, add the sugar and stir on a medium to low heat. Add spices. Mix well and fill into a jam jar for later use. Keep in your fridge and use within a week.

The process of removing the hairy seeds from the rosehips is very time consuming and tedious. You also need a lot of rosehips to just make up one small jar.

Additional information

This recipe refers to a tart in the title but then advises to store the final product in a gallypot. which is a small earthen, usually glazed pot (see picture). This recipe is a classic case of missing some of the important steps – here the cooking, which is absolutely necessary with rosehips. Comparing this recipe with other contemporary rosehip recipes which do let us know that the hips must be boiled until tender, we can conclude that the author made the assumption that the cook would know so anyway. Interesting is the fact that the recipe gives us the option to either use the mixture in a tart for immediate use or keep and preserve some for later.

SAUCE OF GRAPES

Translated, original recipe

> Take blacke grapes and bruse thē in a mortar with some bread,
> according to the quantity you will haue, then temper them with

119

a little Verjuice or Vineger, because the grapes should not be too sweet, then séeth them for the space of halfe an houre with Sinamon, Ginger, and other spice.

Epulario, 1598 translation

Modernised recipe

- Black grapes
- Breadcrumbs to thicken the sauce
- Ground cinnamon, ginger and other spices to taste

Roughly blend the grapes with a hand blender and mix in enough breadcrumbs to achieve a thickish sauce. Add the spices and allow to simmer for about 20-30 minutes. Try serving with fish.

Additional information

Grapes mostly feature in chicken pie recipes in English sixteenth-century cookery, so this recipe being of Italian origin is different.

On 16 September 1532, the gardener of Richmond was rewarded 7s 6d for bringing grapes and pears to the king in 'hamptonco^{r}t'.[29] In 1525 the household accounts of Kenninghall Palace, home of Thomas, Duke of Norfolk, show the acquisition of grapes but no quantities nor price given.[30]

When fresh grapes are called for in recipes, it is mostly in combination with small birds where the coolness of the grapes was believed to counteract the humoral heat of the birds. English recipes also often replace the grapes with gooseberries which were evidently more readily available.

In 1542 Andrew Boorde, usually suspicious of fresh fruit, finds sweet and fresh grapes 'nutrytyue & doth stumulat the flesshe' – very much a thumb's up from him. In *The Haven of Health*, Thomas Cogan is the first to give us the full humoral qualities: sour grapes are cold and moist, sweet grapes hot and moist. Both of them eaten fresh will cause you stomach upset he claims. He also states that grapes are commonly eaten after a meal, which potentially 'corrupts' all the other meat eaten before. In 1599 Henry Butts advises to eat them in moderation with salty meats, pomegranates and vinegar. The best seasons to enjoy them are spring and autumn, and they are recommended for everybody except the elderly.

TO MAKE ALL MANER OF FRUIT TARTE

Transcribed original recipe

> Ou must boyle your fruite, whether it be apple, cherrie, peach, damson, peare, Mulberie, or codling, in faire water, and then they be boyled inough, put them into a bowle, and bruse them with a Ladle, and when they be colde, straine them, and put in red wine or Claret wine, and so season it with sugar, sinnamon and ginger.

The Good Husvvifes Jewell, 1596, Thomas Dawson

Modernised recipe

- ◆ Fresh plums, cut in half with stones removed
- ◆ Red wine
- ◆ Sugar, ground cinnamon and ginger to taste
- ◆ Tart cases, homemade or ready bought.

Boil the fruit in enough water to just cover them. When soft, drain them and remove their skins. Return fruit to the pot. With the back of your ladle squash

them or use a hand blender. Add a little red wine but not so much that it becomes runny. Add sugar and spices and slightly heat mixture to allow the sugar to melt. Fill pastry into tart cases and serve cold.

This fruity paste is also lovely in your porridge or yoghurt.

Additional information

The damson is a subspecies of the plum. In the year 1525, damsons also appear in the household accounts of Kenninghall Palace, once the home of Thomas Duke of Norfolk.[31]

On 1 October 1538 Lady Lisle asks Archdeacon Thomas Thirlby in a letter to remind her on how many pounds of sugar must go to how many pounds of damson or plum.[32] A sure way to force him to respond to her humble request.

Damsons were also welcome food gifts fit for the king. On the 7 August 1530 the gardener of Richmond was rewarded 4s 8d for bringing damsons and filberts for the king at Hampton Court. In August 1532 a poor woman received 3s 4d for bringing damsons to Woodstock for the king.[33]

In *The Haven of Heath* the author, Thomas Cogan, states that plums are cold and moist in the second degree and they are used stewed in wine and in tarts and eaten before dinner. Thomas Muffet, advises to eat damsons not fully ripe boiled or preserved to correct their cold and crude nature. Eaten before dinner or supper they are more of a meal than act as a medicinal dish.

TO BAKE CHICKENS WITH DAMSONS

Transcribed original recipe

Take your Chickens, drawe them and wash them, then breake their bones, and lay them in a platter, then take four handfuls of fine flower, and lay it on a faire boord, put thereto twelve yolks of Egs, a dish of butter, and a litle Saffron: mingle them all together, and make your paste therewith. Then make six coffins, and put in every coffin a lumpe of butter of the bignesse of a Walnut: then season your six coffins with one spoonful of Cloves and Mace, two spoonfuls of Synamon, and one of Sugar, and a spoonful of Salt. Then put your Chickens into your pies: then take Damisons and pare away the outward peele of them, and put twentie in every of your pie, round about your chicken, then put into everie of your coffins, a hand full of Corrans. Then close them up, and put them into the Oven, then let them be there three quarters of an houre.

The Good Huswifes Handmaide for the Kitchin, 1594, anonymous

Modernised recipe

- ◆ Shortcrust paste/pastry made from flour, eggs and butter or ready-made
- ◆ 4-6 chicken breasts (I cut mine into bite-size chunks)
- ◆ Approx. 20 damsons, stones and skin removed
- ◆ 6 spoons of butter
- ◆ Ground cinnamon, cloves, mace, salt and sugar to taste
- ◆ Handful of raisins or currants

Shortcrust paste/pastry:

- ◆ 4 handfuls of flour (possibly more)
- ◆ Approx. 12 egg yolks
- ◆ Approx. 50g butter

Prepare the shortcrust paste with the flour, butter and eggs. Mix and knead until you get the required consistency adding more flour if too wet or a little more butter if too dry.

Cut the pastry into 6 portions, forming 6 little 'coffins' (pie cases) with sturdy walls and a lid. Put a small spoonful of butter into the bottom of each coffin. Add spices and chicken. Surround chicken with damsons and raisins. Close each pie with a pastry lid. Bake in the oven at medium heat until the chicken is properly cooked which takes at least ¾ hour but perhaps even as long 1 ½ hours.

This recipe is worth noting for two reasons, first because it tells you what goes into the shortcrust pastry and secondly it gives rather precise quantities and measures. Both are rarely found in Tudor recipes. I therefore strongly encourage you to follow the measurements here to start with and amend if you have to. Remember, that Tudor eggs were smaller than our modern ones.

Additional information

Dried damson plums are often referred to as prunes. In 1548 William Turner lists the names of plum in in several languages in his *The names of Herbes*.[34] Gerard, like his fellow contemporaries, confirms that damsons 'moisten and cool' and states that he prefers the dried variety and believes the prunes to be healthier.[35] The members of the London Draper's Company had plums bought for 2s 4d and probably turned into pies for their great feast dinner on the first Monday in August 1564.[36]

Plums were also eaten by the sailors on the *Mary Rose* and about 100 plum stones were recovered from the shipwreck.

Robert Dudley, the future Earl of Leicester, bought plums, but he went for the expensive imported 'Genoway' plums which cost him an extravagant 10s per lb. He would have paid a lot less for English-grown plums.[37] Elizabeth would receive the gift of 'boxed plums' from 'Riche' for New Year in 1575.[38]

TARTES OF QUINCES WITHOUT COVERS

Transcribed original recipe

> Straine your Quinces with some wine, when they be boiled tender, and an apple with them, or two or three Wardens, straine them and season them with Sugar, Sinamon and Ginger, and so make tarte without a cover.

A Book of Cookrye, 1591, A.W

Modernised recipe

- ◆ Approx. 2 quinces per person
- ◆ Approx. 100ml white wine
- ◆ 1 hard pear or warden per person
- ◆ ½ apple per person
- ◆ Sugar, cinnamon, ground ginger to taste
- ◆ Pastry cases (homemade or ready-bought)

Peel and core quinces, pears and apple. Boil quinces and pears until almost soft, add apple and boil until all are soft. Strain fruit (drain and mash) and add a little wine. Season with sugar and spices. Fill fruit mash into pastry cases and serve hot or cold.

Additional information

Quince features frequently in all sorts of food related records, from purchases to food gifts.

Robert Dudley purchased high-value fruits frequently, but he also bought quinces at 2s 6d per lb.[39] He also received gifts of quinces: on 28 December 1584 Mrs Barrett's man was rewarded 10s for presenting preserved quinces to 'his lordship'.[40]

One of the more unusual mentions of quince dates to the first October 1538, in a letter to Archdeacon Thomas Thirlby, Lady Lisle uses a rather bizarre 'chat-up' line in that she asks him to remind her of the ratio of how much sugar to quinces is necessary for preserving purposes.[41]

In 1597 Gerard describes the process of making marmalade and recommends quince jelly. He informs us that the quince is cold and dry in the second degree and will produce intelligent children when the mother eats plenty of quinces during her pregnancy.[42]

TO BAKE QUINCE PIES

Transcribed original recipe

> Pare them and take out all the Core: then perboyle them in water till they bee tender: Then take them foorth: and let the water runne from them till they be drie. Then put into everie Quince, Sugar, sinamon and ginger, and fill everie pie there

with, and thē you may let them bake the space of an houre, and so serve them.

The Good Huswifes Handmaide for the Kitchin, 1594, anonymous

Modernised recipe

- ◆ Short pastry (homemade or ready-bought)
- ◆ Approx. 2 quinces per person
- ◆ Sugar, cinnamon and ground ginger to your taste

Peel and decore all quinces. Parboil until soft and drain. Allow to cool. Line pie dish with pastry (keep enough for lid). Add quinces and sprinkle with sugar, cinnamon and ginger. Place pastry lid on top. Bake in the oven at medium heat for circa one hour and remove when pastry is cooked all through.

Additional information

Quinces were considered one of the healthiest and most useful fruits in Tudor England. They were commonly cooked in their natural state as they are too hard to eat raw. Most recipes call for them to be baked in a pie such as this recipe.

Quince pies were always very welcome at all levels in society and indeed most desirable food gifts.

In 1534 Lady Sidney's servant was rewarded 6s 8d for bringing quince pies to the court.[43] In 1563,1564 and 1567 for New Year, Elizabeth was presented with a 'Quince Pye' by John Bettis Seriaunte (sargent) of the Pastrye. By 1571, her new 'Sergaunt of the pastrey', John Dudley, gave her a 'pye of Quinces'. From 1577 the quince pies seem to also have wardens or oranges in them and are being logged as 'faire' or great. In 1584 the 'sergiant of the pasterie', John Dudley, applied even more creativity than usual by making the pies into the letters 'E' and 'R'. By 1599 John Dudley's position was given to Thomas Frenche who still supplied the obligatory 'Pye of Quynces'.[44]

On 15 November 1569, at their first Quarter Dinner, the London Draper's Company spent 22s 8d for eight quince pies.[45] In 1542 Andrew Boorde claimed that baked quince with the core pulled out preserves a man from drunkenness!

Thomas Muffet states that there are two kinds of quince: apple-shaped and pear-shaped. In his opinion they are very wholesome when baked, roasted or made into marmalade and should always be eaten after dinner or supper. Quinces are cold in first degree and dry in the second. In *The Haven of Health* the author, Thomas Cogan, states that quince should not be eaten raw but roasted, stewed, or baked they come highly regarded. He also says that quinces made into *conserva*, prepared in syrup *condite* or made into marmalade they make the perfect medicine for students.

TO BAKE PIPPINS

Transcribed original recipe

> Take your pippins and pare them, and make your coffin of fine paste, then cast a little sugar in the bottomme of the pie. Then put in your Pippins, and set them as close as ye can: then take sugar, sinamon, and Ginger, and make them in a dredge, and fill the Pie therewith: so close it, and let it bake two hours but the Oven must not be too hot.

The Good Huswifes Handmaide for the Kitchin, 1594, anonymous

Modernised recipe

- ♦ About 6 medium sized pippin apples (I used London Pippins)
- ♦ Short pastry (ready-made or homemade)
- ♦ Ground cinnamon, ground ginger and sugar to taste

Grease and flour your pie dish. Line it with your pastry and leave enough to cut a lid. Peel and chop your apples into small slices or rings. Sprinkle sugar onto the bottom of your pie and then arrange the apples evenly, making sure that the bottom is covered. Sprinkle more sugar, cinnamon and ginger over the apples and close your pie with the lid. Bake in the oven at medium heat for about 1½ hours or until done.

Additional information

The word pippin means an apple tree that originated as a seedling, not a grafted tree. The London Pippin was first recorded in 1580 and is believed to originate either from Norfolk or Essex. Pippins are the most mentioned apple types in Tudor recipes and appear by name in numerous account books and household expenses. For the *View Dinner*l, kept in the hall by the London Drapers' Company on 15 March 1563, four pippin pies were noted to have been purchased.[46]

Pippins were also sent to the king as a present. On 8 February 1531, a 'costard mongar' was rewarded 6s 8d for bringing 'pepyns to the king grace'.[47]

They are fairly sweet, typically late-ripening with a fine flavour and generally keep well, which was also highly valued in Tudor times.

TO MAKE AN APPLE MOISE

Transcribed original recipe

Roste your Apples very fair, and when you have so doon, peele
them and strain them with the yolk of an Egge or twaine, and
Rosewater, and boile it on a Chafingdish or Coles with a peece of
sweet Butter, put in sugar and ginger, and when you lay it in your
dish, cast sinamon & Sugar on it'

A Book of Cookrye, 1591, A.W.

Modernised recipe

- ◆ Approx. 5 apples
- ◆ 1-2 egg yolks
- ◆ A few drops of rosewater, to your taste
- ◆ Approx. 10g unsalted butter
- ◆ Sugar to taste
- ◆ Ground ginger to taste
- ◆ Ground cinnamon to taste

Roast the apples in the oven until soft. Remove from oven, allow to cool and peel. Remove core. Mash them. Add egg yolks, rosewater and allow to boil on low heat in a pot for a few minutes. Add butter, sugar and ginger. Stir and allow to simmer until sugar has been dissolved. Serve in pretty dishes and sprinkle a little ground cinnamon on top.

Additional information

Medieval records give us an insight in the value of the apple. In a fruiter's bill of 1292 ordinary apples were 3d and 100 of the costard type set you back 1s.

Apples were not just used as food but there are several cases when they were used as payment in kind as in the example from 1315 at the Runham Estate in Norfolk when a yearly rent was paid with 200 pearmain apples.

Gerard tells us that in Hereford there is a master whose servants drink nothing but apple juice. He clearly prefers the 'corrected' version – boiled or roasted and spices added – to the raw, naturally cold and moist apple.[48]

Apples appear frequently in household accounts as purchased or given as a gift. The Norwich Chamberlains' accounts for 1544 show 16d paid for apples used for a 'banket made in the ffeld without Seynt Stephyns gates on Ester Wedynsday for my lord of Norff' takyn musters ther'.[49]

Cromwell's personal accounts from 1537 show that 40s were paid to Henry Thomas for bringing apples on 3 May. In his 'remembrances' from 1538, there is an entry for 10 December for 7s 6d paid to 'Bowcher' of the Privy Chamber for bringing apples from the King.[50] The king was also a receiver of such apple gifts himself. On 4 April 1530 he rewarded Lady 'Boulstrod's servant 12d for bringing apples.[51]

Robert Dudley, Earl of Leicester's household accounts show 3s 4d paid to a 'power' (probably 'poorer') woman of Hatfield for bringing apples.[52] In 1542 Andrew Boorde said about 'appulles' that they are good if they have been exposed to frost or old apples. He prefers red apples and also suggests eating them with sugar or comfits (sugar-coated fennel or aniseeds). In his opinion, roasted or baked apples are the healthiest. Thomas Elyot elaborates more on the topic of apples in his book *The Castel of Helth*. He agrees that old apples are better as freshly picked ones are cold and hard to digest. He recommends storing them for at least until the next winter or the year after.

Thomas Muffet states that apples shall be eaten at the beginning of a meal but sour ones at the end. All apples are to be avoided being consumed raw and best baked or preserved. None of them are good for cooking except for codlins. These are the turned into tarts and their coldness and 'watrishness' corrected with baking, roasting or preserving with cinnamon, ginger sugar, rosewater, orange peels, aniseed, caraway seed and sweet fennel seed.

In 1599 Henry Butts elaborates that sweet apples are hot in the first degree, but temperately moist sour apples are cold and dry. He recommends apples for young people in spring and autumn.

TO BAKE PEARES, QUINCES, AND WARDENS (*APPLES)

Transcribed original recipe

> You must take and pare them, and then coare them: then make your paste with faire water and Butter, and the yolke of an Egge, and sette your orenges into the paste, and then bake it well: Then fill your paste almost ful with Sinamon, Ginger and Sugar: also apples(*) must be taken after the same sort, saving that whereas the core should be cut out they must be filled with butter everie one: the hardest apples are the best, and like wise are Pears and wardens, and none of them all but the Wardens may be perboiled, and the oven must be of a temperate heat, two hours to stand enough.

> *The Good Huswifes Handmaide for the Kitchin*, 1594, anonymous

Modernised recipe

- ◆ Short, hard pears, preferably wardens (peeled, decored), enough to fill your deep pie dish
- ◆ Candied orange peel, enough to cover the floor of your pie
- ◆ Shortcrust pastry (ready-made) or make your own
- ◆ Sugar, ground cinnamon and ginger to taste
- ◆ Unsalted butter, one spoonful per pear

Shortcrust, if you make your own:

- ◆ Flour
- ◆ Unsalted butter (cubed, room-temperature)
- ◆ 1 egg yolk

Prepare the shortcrust pastry using flour, salt and egg yolk. Combine all ingredients with water and knead into a manageable, fairly dry but strong pastry.

Form a pie bottom and add the sides from your bought or homemade pastry. You want a strong, tall pie dish that can hold pears standing up. The sides are strong enough if they don't need a baking dish for support.

Cover the pie bottom with candied orange peel. Strew sugar and spices on top. Place the peeled and cored whole pears inside the pie – standing up. Fill the pears with butter. Close with a pastry lid if you wish. I filled the gaps between the whole pears with a mixture of orange peels and chopped pear. Place the pie on a greased baking tray. Bake at medium heat for around two hours but keep checking the progress in case too much pear juice is trying to escape messing up your oven!

Additional information

A warden is basically a firm-textured cooking pear that keeps well over the winter, a quality highly appreciated in times when food preservation was very limited.

Although the pear has never been as popular as the apple, these long-lived trees have a long history in England. In 1530 Cardinal Wolsey is reputed to have been eating roasted wardens at the moment when he was seized with his fatal illness.[53] Harris, fruiterer to Henry VIII, introduced pears from France and the low countries in 1533 for the orchard at *Teynham* (Kent).[54] William Shakespeare does not appear to have enjoyed the pear, as most of his references do not appear favourable.

General storage advice was given in the Second Book, *Entreating the ordering of Orchards* (1577) by Conrad Heresbach: in sand, flocks (scraps of wool), covered with wheat or chaff or dipping the stalks in boiling pitch and then hang the pears up. Keeping the pears in freshly boiled wine was another.[55]

TO MAKE WARDENS IN CONSERUE

Transcribed original recipe

> Fyrste make the syrope in this wyse, take a quarte of good romney, and putte a pynte of claryfyedhoney, a pounde of a halfe of suger,and myngle all those together ouer the fyre, tyll tyme they seeth, and then set it to cole. And thys is a good sirop for manye things, and wyll be kepte a yeare or two.Then take thy warden and scrape cleane awaye the barke, but pare them not, and seeth them in a good redde wyne so that they be wel so ked and tender, that the wyne be nere hade soked into them, then take and strayne them through a cloth or through a strayner into a vessel,

then put to them of this syrope asoresayde tyll it be almost fylled, and then caste in the pouders, as syne canel, synamon, pouder of ginger, and such other, put in a boxes, and kepe it yf thou wylt, and make thy Syrope as thou wylt worke in quantyte, as yf thou wylt worke twenty wardens or more, or lesse, as by experience.

A Proper Newe Booke of Cokerye, 1557 edition, anonymous

Modernised recipe

- ◆ 2 pears per person if recipe is being used as a dessert
- ◆ Greek wine (for Romney), 125ml
- ◆ Clear, runny honey, 60ml
- ◆ Sugar, 55g
- ◆ Ground cinnamon, ginger and other spice of your choice, amount to your taste

For cooking the pears

- ◆ Red wine, enough to submerge the pears

I have used the original measurements from this recipe and roughly quartered them for one person.

Syrup

Mix wine, honey and sugar and heat in a pan. Stir until sugar is dissolved and remove from the heat.

Cooking the pears

Peel the pears and remove the core but do not cut them. Cook until they are fairly soft and you can cut them with a spoon. Remove from the heat. Strain half of the pears through a sieve or use a blender. Keep the others for serving up as a dessert (my variation – not part of the original recipe). Mix the mashed pears with the syrup made earlier and add any more spices or sugar if you wish. Place the cooked pears into the centre of your dessert dish and scoop the syrup over the fruit to give it a glazed appearance.

In Tudor times this mixture would we have been cooked longer to allow almost all the fluid to evaporate. The sticky, thick, fruit paste would have been filled into wooden boxes and so kept for a year.

Additional information

Pears were a popular gift to the nobility from commoners, as recorded on 15 December 1534 when Thomas Cromwell received wardens from Sir Henry Penago, and on 2 April 1539 the accounts show an entry of 12d given to a poor woman for bringing wardens.[56] On 10 August 1530 the gardener of Hampton court was paid 7s 5d for bringing pears.[57] The account of William Chancy for Robert Dudley shows a payment of 2s 4d to Parker for the carriage of one brace wardens out of Norfolk in January 1558.[58] On 311538 the aldermen Augustine Steward and Edward Reed were dispatched to Kenninghall in Norfolk to 'haue hys graces will & pleasure iff the cominaltie shall make sute to the kynges grace to haue the graunte off the Blak Freres hous'. The chamberlains equipped them with plenty of drink, gifts and 200 pears.[59]

The health benefits of the (cooked) pear and warden were acknowledged by Andrew Boorde who said in his *Dyetary of Helth* published in 1542 that they were nutritious roasted, stewed or baked and comforted the stomach – especially if eaten with comfits.

In 1599 Henry Butts states in his book *Dyets Dry Dinner* that pears are cold in the first and dry in the second degree which makes them suitable for all but the aged in autumn and winter. He also recommends eating them after a meal with much sugar and old wine.

Chapter 4

WINTER

Food in Winter

Winter in Tudor England was experienced very differently depending on your social status. For the poorest without a home, constantly having to beg and therefore breaking the law, winter was the harshest time of year, while at the other end of society it was the season that offered several excuses for lavish feasts and banquets.

William Harrison, in his contemporary account of Tudor social life *The Description of England* (1587), recognises that people in England needed more food to cope with the cooler weather in winter compared to hotter European countries[1]. In Tudor England that meant drying food, packing it into salt, honey or sugar, or pickling it in vinegar. Fruit that could be stored for several months, such as apples and wardens, as well as root vegetables, remained outside. These were a true winter staple for the less well-off and proved life-saving food in a time of scarcity. This made cabbage, parsnip and leeks so essential for the feeding of a nation.

Most people had a kitchen garden and reserved some seeds for sowing in the autumn in order to have a winter supply of radishes, lamb's lettuce, carrots, turnips, spinach, sorrel and onions. This meant that people in the countryside did not need to go without roots or greenstuff in winter.

Certain preserved food, in particular packed in salt, tended to be only used in winter, such as poor Johns and dried, salted fish. While the poor were lucky to add some stockfish or salted bacon to their daily pottage in winter, the nobility and upper class feasted on wildfowl and game, often served as a pie.

Even in the late sixteenth century, food preservation for winter was at the top of everybody's agenda. While the common people mostly used vinegar and salt, the upper class went into a new trend: fruit preservation with sugar. Authors of cookery books and printers were quick to jump on the bandwagon and cash in on the willingness of England's ladies to get their fingers sticky, quite literally.

Thomas Tusser advises his readership in 1557 as part of this book *Five Hundred Points of Good Husbandry* in the January abstract: 'Bid Christmas adieu, thy stock now renew'.[2] Sir Thomas Elyot (1490-1545) explains in his book *The Castel of Helth* how to go about it. As winter increases 'phlegm' due to the rain and dampness of the season, as well as the longer nights, all meats ought to be roasted rather than boiled. Meat and fish should be finely minced, and all fresh fruit should be avoided. Roasted or baked quince is allowed and so is sweet red wine. He reminds his readership that in winter one needs to eat more than in summer and that winter is the enemy of older people. He states the 8 November as the beginning of winter and 8 February as the end.

The Elizabethan physician Thomas Cogan also attributes cold and moist characteristics to winter and recommends eating beef and pork as they provide the necessary increased substance. Herbs and raw fruit are to be 'refused' at all times.

Food at Christmas in Tudor Times

Before the Reformation, advent, or the Forty days of St Martin, was a period of fasting which ended on Christmas Eve. Celebrations and festive food started to be served for twelve days known as Christmastide.

Between the fourth Sunday after the nativity and Christmas Day the diet was restricted to soups, stews and fish instead of roasts and pies for the wealthy. The poor classes would have found the reduction of food at this time of year a real misery and in the fourteenth century James Ryman complained of eating 'no puddings nor sauce but stinking fish not worth a louse'.[3]

Christmas was a time when, by tradition, the wealthier members of society were supposed to extend their hospitality to those less fortunate. In 1557 Thomas Tusser reminds his readership of those suffering:

> At Christmas, the hardness of winter doth rage,
> A griper of all things, and specially age:
> Then lightly poor people, the young with the old,
> Be sorest oppressed with hunger and cold
> At Christmas, by labour is little to get,
> That wanting, - the poorest in danger are set:
> What season then better, of all the whole year,
> Thy needy, poor neighbour to comfort and cheer[4]

Advent fasting meant no meat, cheese, milk or eggs and included Christmas Eve. After such a long time of food restrictions, the first feast on Christmas Day would have been very welcome.

Christmas Day was an occasion for generosity. The wealthy mostly entertained their social equals such as neighbours and sometimes tenants, but the landlord was obliged to throw a feast for his tenants. In return they were expected to bring gifts, which were mostly farm produce.

The custom of eating high-value meats and other luxurious foods continued at Christmas and survived the test of time as well as the influence of the Reformation.

Venison was the meat of the nobility and generally could not be purchased – you either were 'gifted' it or you had your own deer park, a so-called forest which supplied you with both hunting fun and venison meat. Christmas fell right into the hunting season and so venison was clearly a popular choice. Most recipes call for boiled or roasted venison and baked in a pie. Tudor physician and former Carthusian monk Andrew Boorde esteemed it 'gentlemen's food' and felt that nowhere in the world was venison so esteemed as in England.

Some meats such as chicken and rabbit were subject to price hiking in the run up to Christmas before dipping to well below average during Lent. English household accounts between 1500 and 1600 also reveal that sausage was also becoming more popular with the gentry at Christmas. It has to be also noted that some vegetables became increasingly more popular in the late sixteenth century, and this is reflected in household accounts and cookery books aimed at the well-to-do. A popular vegetable was the turnip, purchased during the cold season.

Plum porridge, later known as plum pudding, was a thick broth of mutton or beef with plums, bread, spices, dried fruit and wine in Tudor times. During Elizabeth's reign, flour started to be added. Figgy pudding was a kind of sweet dish made from almonds, wine, figs, raisins, ginger and honey. Brawn was very salty pork or boar and served with mustard. Brawn was the Christmas dish available to most people. Andrew Boorde calls it the usual meat in winter amongst Englishmen.

Turkey started to appear in England during the sixteenth century. The earliest record is about six birds imported and sold at Bristol for 2d in 1526. The new arrival began to be recognised during the 1530s, sold at markets in 1540s, and by the end of the 1500s started to appear as Christmas food. Stuffing, known as forcemeat, contained egg, currants, pork and herbs and was first recorded served with poultry in 1538.[5]

Brussel sprouts were first recorded in 1587 in Europe but there is no English recipe or record from the sixteenth century, and it is very doubtful that they featured as part of a Tudor Christmas dinner.

Twelfth (Night) cake was a type of sweetbread with spices and dried fruit but sadly no original recipe from the 1500s survives.

Bean cake appears to be some kind of gingerbread and was also known as peppercake. Inside there was a coin or bean and sometimes also a pea. The couple who received the slice containing the bean and the pea were made King and Queen of the Bean and led the singing and dancing.

Lambs Wool in a Wassail Bowl is a spiced ale-based seasonal Christmas drink with floating roasted crab apples. The word wassail occurs in extracts from Spenser, Shakespeare and Ben Johnson.

Boar's head is mostly associated with Queen's College in Oxford where it has been served since 1341. A boar's head is a true status symbol and the king of France once sent Henry a Christmas gift of wild boar paté.

Frumenty was an extremely popular side dish served with venison. Frumenty is wheat boiled in milk or ale with eggs, fruit, spices and sometimes sugar, cream or almond milk.

No feast went without its banquet and that was true for Christmas too. 'Banqueting stuffe' was the dessert course consisting of sweetmeats, and diverse canapés such as suckets, comfits, marchpane, sweetbreads and biskets.

Food as gifts in Tudor England

At Christmas the traditional giving of food in the form of a hamper is still very much a popular choice today, together with the obligatory box of chocolates and a bottle of wine. In Tudor England the exchange of food gifts was a means of maintaining relationships. In an age when not everybody was able to write, this exchange provided a sense of community and intimacy that otherwise would have been difficult to sustain.

Various items of food were given as gifts between families, communities, companies and guilds as well as within aristocratic circles. The Tudors did not celebrate birthdays with presents, but gifts of food given throughout the year created bonds and might have formed an accompaniment to negotiations in the short or long term. The importance of social connection could be expressed in these bonds arising from the humble gifts of food. Those gifts, however, might link to eternal responsibilities and obligations.

Rewards paid to people for bringing gifts of food illustrate the role that this could play in supplying certain items. All received gifts were carefully recorded together with the payment disbursed to the giver, as the giving of an item in Tudor England was always considered a part of an 'exchange' and that exchange could be the winning of a favour. In some way this was a little bit like the recording of Christmas cards received and sent out in return the year after. To have your gift returned or not receiving anything in return was the most powerful way to publicly humiliate the giver, as was the case when Henry VIII deliberately made no gift to Catherine of Aragon on New Year's Eve in 1532.

Food given as alms for the needy was a routine part of life in a great household, especially at Christmas when Lords of the manor were meant to open their doors to the poor on their estate and provide them with a cooked meal. Gifts of chickens, capons, meat pies and tarts appear fairly frequently in account and household books. Exotic imports such as turkey, which had been introduced to England in the 1520s but not a common sight until the 1570s, featured highly on the list of prestigious food gifts.

Food gifts, particularly those from hunting and fishing expeditions, were a mark of special favour, as these foods had sumptuary characteristics. By the sixteenth century there were legal restrictions in place on taking beasts of the chase and game. Customary practice restricted access to some foods, for example wild birds.

Venison was also highly prized and commonly reserved for royalty and those who owned a deer park, making it a highly regarded gift of food. William Harrison felt that deer parks (forests) were of little profit to their owners since they could not sell the deer and often ended up giving it away as a present. There are numerous entries in the *Dinner Book of the London Drapers' Company* for venison, but the money spent appears to be rewards, an indication that the deer was 'gifted' rather than bought.

Royalty and aristocracy attracted luxury food gifts and the giver would win favour if the gift was accepted. These gifts, such as game and exotic fruit as well as spices, were part of a social currency. Prestigious foods were always welcome, marking status and bestowing honour on both the donor and the recipient. In the letters of the famous Norfolk based family the Pastons we notice gifts of swans and cranes being recorded and on one occasion in 1503 there is also a gift of storks.[6]

A monarch would also receive a string of food gifts by commoners wherever they travelled. These gifts tended to be taken from the land and livestock of locals who sent them to the monarch themselves or via a servant. Servants bringing expensive food gifts from their masters were well tipped. Gifts of food for special occasions frequently featured game which always attracted rewards.

There is a clear rise in the number of different garden produce being given as gifts by the end of the sixteenth century. At the beginning of the century, presents of food other than meat or fish were rare and less varied. Sometimes the rarity was the fact that fruit was early or late in the season. Effective storing techniques would make the gift of apples in the spring a real treat.

All sorts of banqueting food, sweetmeats as well as sugar cones, were not only one of the most desired but also the costliest foods one could give. In the account of William Chancy for Robert Dudley from 1558-9, the Earl of

Leicester is the lucky recipient of a sugar cone which was sent via a servant of Sir John York and received a reward of 3s and 5d.[7]

Recipes

<><><><><><><><><><><><><><><><><><><><><><><><><><><><>

TO BAKE PYGEONS IN A SHORT PASTE AS YOU MAKE TO YOURE BAKEN APPLES

Transcribed original recipe

> Season youre pigeons with peper, saffron, cloues and mace, with vergis and salte, then putte them into youre paste, and so close them vp, and bake them, they wyl bake in halfe an houre, then take them for the, and yf ye thinke theym drye, take a little vergis and butter and put in theim and so serue theym.

A Proper Newe Booke of Cokerye, 1557

Modernised recipe

- Pigeon breasts
- Ready-made or homemade shortcrust pastry
- Ground pepper, crushed saffron, ground cloves and mace to taste
- Salt to taste
- Mild apple vinegar to taste
- Butter, if needed

Prepare the pie pastry and line a pie oven dish with your pastry (leaving enough for a lid to be cut). Season the pigeon breasts with the spices and lay them into the pie evenly. Close with pastry lid. Bake at medium heat between 30 minutes and 1 hour. If you think the meat is too dry, add a vinegar/butter mixture through a hole in the lid. Serve hot.

The taste of pigeons is slightly unusual, perhaps a blend of liver and venison. The meat is very lean, and I felt the advice to add butter with vinegar worked well. My family enjoyed this pie and we actually liked the taste of pigeon but most of us would have preferred to have some gravy to go with it.

Additional information

The meat of pigeons was highly esteemed in Tudor England and the cookery book for this recipe advises that pigeons are always in season, but they need to be young.

Pigeons were highly regarded as food gifts in Tudor England. Politician Edward Harley (1624-1700) received a pigeon pie as a luxury gift.[8] Sir

Thomas Elyot praises them for being easily digested and wholesome. In his book *The Haven of Health* Thomas Cogan states that pigeons are very hot and moist in complexion and are best killed when just ready to fly. He claims that cunning cooks have devised 'to stuffe them with grapes' before they get roasted.

PEGIONS STEWED

Transcribed original recipe

> Pegions stewed. To mak pegions stewed hew pegions small and put them in an erthen pot then tak erbes and pilled garlike and chope them to gedur and put them in good brothe put ther to whit grece poudur and vergious colour it with saffron and salt it and stew it well and serue it.

> *A noble book off cookry ffor a prynce houssolde or eny other stately houssolde*, c.1500

Modernised recipe

- ◆ Pigeon fillets
- ◆ Various green, leafy vegetables and herbs of the season
- ◆ Fresh garlic to taste
- ◆ Vegetable or chicken stock, about 1l
- ◆ Saffron (3-4 strands ground)
- ◆ Salt and mild apple vinegar to taste
- ◆ A spoon or two of fat such as goose fat or lard
- ◆ Spices of your choice such as ground ginger, nutmeg, mace, cinnamon, pepper, etc.

Bring stock to boil. Chop pigeon fillets into bite-size chunks. Finely chop leafy vegetables, herbs and garlic. Cook pigeon, vegetable leaves and garlic until meat is tender. Add spices, fat and finely chopped herbs. Allow to cook for another minute or so and serve.

Additional information

This recipe dating to roughly the reign of Henry VII is unusual as it contains garlic, something upper-class cuisine generally avoided. However, of all the Tudor pigeon recipes I have recreated, this is my favourite one.

In Tudor England pigeons were considered one of the healthiest birds to consume – easily digested and beneficial to people with phlegmatic constitutions when eaten in moderation,[9] and for that reason they were often kept in dovecotes for the purpose of being fattened up.

However, the 1587 folio of William Harrison's *The Description of England* states that pigeons are 'now an hurtful fowl by reason of their multitudes and number of houses daily erected for their increase, which the bowers (husbandmen) of the country call in scorn almshouses and dens of thieves and suchlike'.[10] Clearly the pigeon population grew out of control, causing damage to food production.

The elite seem to have been particularly keen on very young birds, which attracted high prices in the marketplace, and squabs (pigeons, taken from their nest at a pre-fledgling stage) may have accounted for some 1,000 pigeons bought over in six months by Sir William Cecil and some of the 200 purchased by Sir Edward Radcliffe.[11]

Young pigeons had a limited season, from late spring until autumn, and could not be purchased outside this time. In William Petre's household in 1552, 1,080 pigeons were consumed between Easter and Michaelmas. Pigeon formed also part of Thomas Howard, Third Duke of Norfolk's funeral in late August 1554.[12]

There was no legal restriction on the killing of pigeons and the keeping of a dovecote was usually a privilege reserved for the lord of the manor.[13]

In 1599, in his book *Dyets Dry Dinner*, Henry Butts recommends pigeons to be boiled in fat flesh broth with vinegar, plums, cherries and coriander. In his opinion it is flesh best suited for the cold weather and for old people.

TO BAKE A TURKEY AND TAKE OUT HIS BONES

Transcribed original recipe

> Take a fat turkey, and after you haue scalded him and washed him cleane, lay him vpon a faire cloth and slit him throughout the backe, and when you haue taken out his garbage then you must take out his bones so bare as you can. When you haue so doone wash him cleane, then trusse him and pricke his backe together, and so haue a faire kettle of seething water and perboyle him a little. Then take him vp that the water may runne cleane out of

him, and when he is colde, season him with pepper and Salt, and then pricke hym with a fewe cloues in the breast, and also drawe him with larde if you like of it, and when you haue maide of your coffin and laide your Turkie in it, then you must put some Butter in it, and so close him vp. in this sorte you may bake a goose, a Pheasant or capon.

The Good Husvvifes Jewell, 1596, Thomas Dawson

Modernised recipe

- ◆ Turkey (cleaned, gutted)
- ◆ Pepper and salt to taste
- ◆ A few cloves
- ◆ Some butter
- ◆ Pastry – enough to enclose your turkey (preferably made without egg or butter but short crust if you prefer to eat the pastry)

Parboil the turkey in water until there is no more raw flesh. Remove and allow to cool down and drain water from it. Stick several cloves into the skin on the breast and season with salt and pepper. Cover your turkey with your flat paste and add some butter. Alternatively lay your baking tin (pre-grease and dust with flour to avoid sticking) with the pastry and put large turkey slices on top. Add a little butter and close up with a pastry lid. Depending on the size of your turkey bake between 2-3 hours. The pre-cooking in water eliminates the risk of the turkey being still raw in places. Serve without the pastry if you have used one without egg but you may choose to eat the pastry if you have opted to use short pastry.

This recipe is also suitable for using 'leftover' Turkey.

Additional information

Turkey was also known as 'Turkish chickens' or 'Indian chickens'.

The name 'turkey' came from the widespread misapprehension that it came from the east, via the country of Turkey, but that was a different bird, the guinea fowl (from the same family), which was native to sub-Saharan Africa and reintroduced to Europe in the fifteenth century by the ethnically Turkish Mamluks.[14]

The turkey arrived in Europe between 1523-24. It soon became a domesticated fowl in the 1530s and was widely sold in markets from the 1540s, and by 1555 the price of turkeys was legally fixed in the London market.

A young trader by the name of William Strickland who sailed to the New World with the Venetian explorer Sebastian Cabot is often credited with the introduction of turkey to England, but this is not really possible as he was only born in around 1530. However, he was granted a coat of arms that featured 'a turkeycock in his pride proper' in 1550.[15]

Towards the end of the sixteenth century turkey was beginning to replace peacock and swan as the centrepiece of feasts and made an appearance at Christmas dinners. In the 1560s the Duke of Northumberland's household menu contained not just a swan but a goose and a 'turkie'.

Probate inventories usually named birds as 'pullen', but turkeys began to be itemised separately – noticeably in East Anglia and Hampshire. Anne Arminger was a widow of North Creake in Norfolk in the early sixteenth century and owned two turkey cocks and three turkey hens. Turkeys bred in East Anglia were walked to London for sale at the markets there.[16]

Stuffing with meat, known as forcemeat, and made with egg, currants, pork and herbs, is first known to have been served with poultry in 1538. Thomas Tusser, author of *Five Hundred Points of Good Husbandry*, published in 1557 mentions the turkey in context with Christmas in the 1577 edition:

> Good husband and huswife, now cheefly be glad,
> things handsom to haue, as they ought to be had,
> They both doo prouide against CHRISTMAS doo come,
> to welcome good neighbour, good cheer to haue some;
>
> Good bread and good drinke, a good fier in the hall,
> Brawn, pudding and souse, and good mustard withall.
>
> Beefe, mutton, and porke, shred pies of the best,
> pig, veal, goose, and capon, and **turkey** well drest;
>
> Cheese, apples, and nuts, ioly Carols to heare,
> as then in the countrie is counted good cheare.
>
> What cost to good husband is any of this,
> good houshold prouision onely it is;
> Of other the like, I doo leaue out a menie,
> that costeth the husbandman neuer a penie[17]

The earliest record for a turkey supplied to the rather wealthy London Draper's Company for their dinners shows an entry in 1564 for one turkey cock costing

5s, however this potentially could also refer to the smaller guinea fowl, then also known as 'turkey'.[18]

The gifting of luxurious turkey to judges, an attempt to buy their favour, was also not an uncommon act of 'kindness'. Between July 1596 and March 1601 turkey appears on the list of many food gifts for the two country gentlemen judges Thomas Walmsey and Edward Fenner.[19] However, despite their rapidly growing popularity, this new addition to the dinner table of the wealthy also attracted a degree of prejudice against the new meat. William Harrison, in his *Description of England* in 1587, expressed his objection to 'rankness' and the strong taste of the turkey, or the Indish peacocks as he also calls them, by gelding the birds.[20]

TO MAKE SAUCE FOR CAPONS OR TURKIE FOULES

Transcribed original recipe text

> To make sauce for Capons or Turkie Foules. Take Onions, slice them thin, boil them in faire water til they be boyled drie, put some of the gravy unto them, + pepper grose beaten.

The Good Huswifes Handmaide for the Kitchin, 1594, anonymous

Modernised recipe

- ◆ Roast turkey
- ◆ Onions, peeled and sliced
- ◆ Coarsely ground black pepper to taste
- ◆ Some of the fat and juice gathered during the roasting process of the turkey.

Roast your turkey and collect all fat and juice in the process. Boil onion slices in a little water until all fluid has evaporated. Add some 'gravy' (fat and juices gathered from roasting the turkey) and add pepper. Return to heat and boil for a minute or two. Put mixture on a serving plate and place turkey pieces on top. Serve hot.

Additional information

Turkey probably arrived in Europe from Central America in the 1520s. Archbishop Cranmer listed it as a great bird for the table in 1541 and over the following years it effectively replaced the peacock as a main item of poultry.[21]

Turkey became very popular amongst the English very quickly and was also a desirable food gift. On 26 July 1596 presents received at Launceston for the Judges of Assize Riding the Western and Oxford Circuits included two turkeys.[22]

The first Tudor physician to comment on turkey is Thomas Muffet who says in *Health's Improvement* that 'turkies' were first brought from 'Turky' to Europe, hence their name. He also mentions the guinea fowl. He calls their flesh 'dainty and worthy of a Princes Table'. They should be killed in the winter, hung for a day and a night before being cooked to be the most wholesome. He recommends putting whole cloves into the skin while roasting. He also approves of baking the meat because it soaks up its 'watrishness'.

By 1599 Henry Butts states that the 'Turky-Cocke or Ginny-Cocke', mixing up the guinea fowl with the turkey, should be allowed to hang in winter for one night before being prepared. In his opinion turkey needs spicing and thoroughly cooking. It is hot and moist in the second degree and can be eaten at any time.

TO ROASTE A QUAILE

Transcribed original recipe

> Let his legs be broken, and knit one within another, and so roaste him
> Sauce for Capons, Feasnts, Partridges, or Woodcockes:

Onions sliced verie thinne, faire water and Pepper grosse
beaten

The Good Huswifes Handaide for the Kitchin, 1594

Modernised recipe

- ◆ 1 quail per person
- ◆ Fresh onions, sliced
- ◆ Ground pepper

Roast the quails until done. The bird is so small that this process does not take long.
Choose medium heat so as not to burn it. Prepare the sauce by briefly cooking the
onion in very little water. Add pepper and serve the quail on the bed of onion.

The simplicity of this recipe works really well to bring out the delicate
flavour of the quail.

Additional information

A Proper Newe Boke of Cokerye from 1545 states that the quail is always in
season.

Quail was considered unhealthy, but just like chocolate today, people totally ignored the warning and celebrated this bird as a dainty dish instead.[23] In 1542 Andrew Boorde says that quails 'nouryshynges' very little and they are likely to cause depression. This view is also held by Sir Thomas Elyot who states that some people eat it anyway.

In *Health's Improvement* Thomas Muffet explains that quail had such a poor reputation because they were accused of eating hemlock and hellebore, which are both toxic to humans. He bemoans that in spring and summer quails are too dry and in autumn and winter they are too moist. In his opinion they are only good young, before they start feeding on those poisonous plants. Thomas Cogan, on the other hand, claims that quails are wholesome and states that they were the 'meate that God rained from heaven to feed the Israelites withal in the desert'. In 1599 Henry Butts still repeats the opinion of the earlier commentators, but he adds that they should be eaten with vinegar and coriander. Quail is hot in the end of the first and moist in the end of the second degree, Butts shares.

Henry VIII's third wife, Jane Seymour, is known to have craved quail during her pregnancy in May 1537, and, luckily for her, Lord and Lady Lisle were able to source them from Calais. In a letter from John Husee to Lady Lisle dated 24 May 1537, he thanks her for the quails in the name of the king who commanded half of them to be roasted straight away.[24] On 21 May 1544 Henry VIII ordered in a proclamation that quails should be sold at 4s per dozen.[25]

The account of William Chancy for Robert Dudley, Earl of Leicester shows several payments for the purchase of quail.[26] *The Dinner Book of the London Drapers' Company* shows that for their Feast Dinner on the first Monday in August 1565, ten dozen of quails were purchased from Mr Warden Renolds.[27]

Quails also feature as bribe-gifts. The Expenses of the Judges of Assize Riding the Western and Oxford Circuits list quails donated at Dorchester by Mr Uvedale with a value of 6d.[28]

TO BAKE CHICKENS IN WINTER

Transcribed original recipe text

> Cut off their feet, and truss them, and put them in the pies, take to everie pie a certain of Corrans or Prunes, and put them in the pie with the Chickens. Then take a good quantitie of Butter to every chicken, and put in the pie: then take a good quantitie of ginger and salt, and season them together, and put them in the pie, let it bake the space of an houre and a halfe, when they be baken take sauce as is aforesaid, and so serve them in.

[...] and to make syrrope for the same pie, take Malmsey, Creame, and two yolkes of Egges, and beat them together, and put in Synamon and Sugar, and when the Pie is almost baked, then put in the syrrop, and let them bake together.

The Good Huswifes Handmaide for the Kitchin, 1594

Modernised recipe

- Short pastry (readymade or homemade)
- Chicken fillets
- Handful of currants or finely chopped prunes
- 1-2 spoons of butter
- Ground ginger and salt to taste
- 1 cup of malmsey wine (fortified, sweet, rich white wine from Madeira)
- Half a cup of cream
- 2 egg yolks
- Cinnamon and sugar to taste

Line your pie dish with the pastry. Cut chicken into bite-size chunks and lay out on pastry evenly. Add the currants (or prunes), butter, ginger and salt. Close with a

153

pastry lid and bake in a medium hot oven for about 1½ hours or until done. Remove from the oven and make a small hole in the pastry lid. Mix the wine, cream the two yolks, cinnamon and sugar and pour this into your pie through the hole. Return to the oven for another few minutes until the yolk has had a chance to set. Serve hot.

Additional information

English historical tradition associates malmsey 'malvesy' wine with the death of George Plantagenet, Duke of Clarence, brother of King Edward IV of England. Following his conviction for treason, he was privately executed on 18 February 1478, and soon after this event the rumour gained ground that he was drowned in a butt of malmsey wine.

To cut up a hen in front of dinner guests was called 'to spoil' it, and to cut up a chicken was known as to 'fruche' it.[29] The proverb 'as tender as a chicken' dates to 1678.[30]

HOW TO SEETH HENNES AND CAPONS IN WINTER IN WHITE BROTH

Transcribed original recipe text

> Take a necke of mutton and a marrowe bone, and let them boile with the Hens together, then take Carret rootes and put them into the potte, and then straine a little bread to thicke the pot with all and not too thicke: season it with Pepper and Vergious, and then cover them close, and then let them boile together, then cut sops and put the broth and the marrow above, and so serve them.

The Good Huswifes Handmaide for the Kitchin, 1594

Modernised recipe

- ◆ Neck of mutton (or lamb), whole
- ◆ Marrow bone
- ◆ Chicken breast (whole)
- ◆ A few carrots, peeled and sliced
- ◆ Handful of breadcrumbs
- ◆ Pepper and apple vinegar to taste
- ◆ Slice of toasted bread

Cook the mutton, the marrow bone and the chicken all in the same pot until almost done. Add the carrots and cook until they are soft. Add breadcrumbs and season with pepper and apple vinegar and cook the broth with the lid on for another half an hour on low heat. Put toasted bread in into the serving dish. Remove meat from broth, cut into a bite size chunks and arrange on top of the bread. Pour the rest of the broth over it and serve.

Additional information

To cut a capon was referred to as to 'sauce' a capon as we learn from Wynkyn de Worde's *The Boke of Keruynge* from 1508.

SAUCE FOR A GOOSE

Transcribed original recipe text

> Sauce for a Gooce. Take Vineger and appells shred very small, two spoonulls of mustard a lit- Pepper and Salte: and take Suger sufficient to sweeten it, then boyle it well together.

> *The Good Hous-wiues Treasurie*, 1588, anonymous

Modernised recipe

- ◆ 1 roast goose
- ◆ Mild apple vinegar, approx. 1 cup
- ◆ Some apples, peeled and chopped
- ◆ 2-3 spoonfuls of mustard
- ◆ Pepper and salt to taste
- ◆ Sugar to taste

Put all ingredients in a pot and allow the apples to cook until soft. If you find the vinegar flavour too strong add more water. Serve hot with your roast goose. The sharp sauce complements the goose perfectly.

Additional information

The carving of a goose was known as 'to rear'. In England, before the arrival of the turkey, goose was the main poultry served up at Christmas. It was also the traditional meal on the church holidays Whitsuntide and Michaelmas.

Physicians considered the meat hard and coarse and difficult to digest. According to the advice given in *A Proper Newe Booke of Cokerye* from 1557, geese were best eaten young, often referred to as 'green' geese – under four months old.

Thomas Cogan informs in his book *The Haven of Health* that 'green' (young) geese are better than stubble ones and tame geese are to be preferred over wild geese. In *Health's Improvement* Thomas Muffet advises to eat the pleasant and sweet flesh of a goose with sorrel sauce to correct its malignity.

Geese were also popular gift foods and Sabine Johnson, the wife of successful merchant John Johnson, often sent goose to friends as a 'remembrance'.[31] Robert Dudley received a 'guse' from Mrs Notes on 20 September 1585 for which she was rewarded 2s and 6d.[32]

Goose and goose pie were also popular 'gifts' for the Judges of Assize Riding the Western and Oxford Circuits. At the spring assizes of the same judges, which began at Andover on 20 February 1597, Mr Sheriff gifted one goose pie amongst other food stuff. [33] However, it was still good enough to be gifted to the king, as one record from December 1531 shows. The servant of the treasurer was rewarded 5s for bringing a capon and a 'gose' to the king.[34] The proverb 'He cannot say Bo(o) to a goose' dates to 1588.[35]

ROSTE A PHEASANT & SAUCE FOR PHEASANT

Transcribed original recipe

> Roste a pheasant. You must roste a pheasant with his head off, his wings and legs on whole and when you serve him in, stick one of his feathers upon his brest.
>
> Sauce for pheasant. Onions sliced very thin, faire water and pepper groce beaten.

A Book of Cookrye, 1591, A.W

Modernised recipe

- 1 pheasant
- 1-2 onions, sliced
- Coarse ground pepper to taste.

Roast your pheasant in the oven at medium heat until done. Ten minutes before it is ready, boil the sliced onions until all the water has evaporated. Season with pepper and put on your serving dish. Place the roast pheasant on top and serve.

Additional information

According to *A Proper Newe Booke of Cokerye* (1557) pheasants are always in season and good to eat but best when taken with a hawk. Together with partridge, pheasants were considered superior to all other wild fowl and most prized on fashionable tables. Pheasants were most commonly caught with hawks making it even more suitable for the dinner table of the nobility. Both birds would have been 'hung' for several days, which allows the meat to become more tender and gives it the distinctive strong flavour so much desired by many.[36]

The records for Henry VIII's Privy Purse Accounts from November 1532 show two payments to the 'fesaunt breder' at 'Elthm' on 16 and 25 November.[37] This probably refers to the French priest who was given the task to start the pheasant breeding project for Henry.

Pheasants rarely feature in purchasing accounts but do appear as food-gifts and, of course, bribery. Judges Thomas Walmsley and Edward Fenner, riding the western and Oxford circuits from February 1597, received four pheasants from Mr Sheriff at Southampton.[38] On 10 December 1538 Dr Layton's servant was rewarded 3s 4d for bringing a pheasant to Thomas Cromwell.[39] Robert Dudley, Earl of Leicester's account books show numerous entries of gifted pheasants. On 18 April 1584, Mr Quarlus' man was rewarded 3s 4d for presenting two 'lyve pheasants' to his lordship.[40] Elizabeth's New Year gifts mostly featured sweet treats but for the year 1559 she was also gifted pheasants by gentleman usher Robert Newort.[41]

Magnificent fowl like pheasants were stereotypically served at court, and pheasant dishes were often 'faked' by womenfolk of middling sort and urban professionals using domestic cookery books such as *The Treasury of Commodious conceits* (1573) to guide them in the process.

In 1542 Andrew Boorde calls pheasants nutritious in his book *A Dyetary of Helth*.

Sir Thomas Elyot also praises the fowl as 'excedeth all fowles in sweetnesse and holsomnesse' in his publication *The Castel of Helth*. This opinion was shared by Thomas Cogan who calls it a 'meate for Princes and great estates and for poore schollers when they can get it' in his book *The Haven of Health*, published in 1584.

Thomas Muffet believes pheasants to be excellent in constitution and claims that all writers prefer it as the soundest and best meat of all other. He recommends pheasants to be eaten in winter and to opt for young ones. He also warns that should ploughmen or 'sabourers' eat pheasants they are likely to suddenly fall sick and suffer from shortness of breath.

SAUCE FOR A MAWLERD ROSTED

Transcribed original recipe

> Sauce for a mawlerd Rosted. Take onyons And mense them wele. Put sum yn thy mawlerd so have the sele And mynce mo Onyons I the ken With the grece of the mawlerd seth hit then Put ale mustard And hony ther to Boyle all to geder tyll hit be enowe.

> *Gentyll manly Cokere*, c.1480-1500

Modernised recipe

- 1 duck
- Onions, minced, 2 portions
- Reserved duck fat from roasting process, 2-3 spoonfuls
- Ale, enough to make sauce
- Mustard, to your taste
- Honey, to your taste

Stuff the duck with minced onions and roast until cooked. Fry the remaining onions with some of the duck fat released into the baking dish whilst roasting. Add the ale, mustard and honey and stir into a smooth sauce. Allow to simmer for a few minutes. Put sauce onto a serving dish and serve the roasted duck on top.

Additional information

In the recipe it says to stuff the duck with onions for good luck which I would translate as 'for good measure'.

During the time of Henry VII's reign, when this recipe was written, ducks and mallards were not regarded as a healthy option to eat unless you were elderly, in which case you would have been encouraged to eat duck. Andrew Boorde valued them only for their feathers but not the meat. His attitude was backed up in a comment he made in 1545 about the Bohemians who, in his words, also found them unpalatable. Generally, they were treated with suspicion and this prejudice against ducks and mallards only started to lift towards the end of the century; perhaps the 'lean' years with constant food shortages had something to do with it. People at the lower end of society would have definitely eaten duck and we also know that during Mary's reign, in 1555/6, imprisoned Protestant clerics and martyrs in Oxford were occasionally offered mallard and teal to eat.

Mallards and Ducks worked also for purchasing favours from the assize judges. On 26 July 1596 the judges Thomas Walmsley and Edward Fenner received two ducks at Launceston from Mr Sheriffe.[42]

TO BAKE A MALLARD

Transcribed original recipe

Take three or foure Onyons, and stampe them in a morter, then straine them with a saucer full of vergice, then take your mallard and put him into the iuyce of the sayde Onyons, and season him with pepper, and salte, cloues and mace, then put your Mallard into the coffin with the saide iuyce of the onyons, and a good quantity of Winter-sauorye, a little tyme, and perselye chopped small, and sweete Butter, so close it vp and bake it.

The Good Husvvifes Iewell, 1596, Thomas Dawson

Modernised recipe

- 3-4 onions, finely chopped
- 1 cup of mild apple vinegar ('vergice')
- 4 mallard duck breasts
- Ground pepper, cloves and mace to taste
- Salt to taste
- Shortcrust pie case (homemade or bought)
- Fresh or frozen parsley, winter savory and thyme – finely chopped and to taste
- A spoonful of unsalted butter

Prepare your 'coffin' by either lining a pie baking dish with your bought pastry or form a strong, thick pie crust from your homemade pastry (approx. 450g plain flour, 250ml warm water, 75g butter). The original recipe strains the liquid from the squeezed onions by pounding them in a mortar first and then straining this mushy texture through a fine sieve. If that sounds like too much work for you, use a hand blender instead but that would get you more 'liquid' than you probably need. The recipe also does not specify whether the pie crust was blind baked before which leaves that decision to you. I did not but allowed for a longer, more temperate baking. I also chopped the duck breasts into bite-size chunks for easier consumption. Make a sort of marinade from your onion mush, pepper, salt, cloves and mace. Apply this marinade evenly all over your meat and place into your pastry case. Add all the herbs and a small number of butter knobs. Close the pie with a pastry lid and bake in your oven at medium heat for at least 1½ hours but it might possibly even take 2 hours. Should you find that the top is already getting dark, but the bottom is not yet fully cooked, return the pie to the oven upside down for another half an hour. Serve hot.

Additional information

Winter/summer savory is a herb which was quite commonly used in Tudor England. Thomas Cogan advises in 1584 of the herb's medicinal benefits and states that it is best dried and made into powder. Savoury is hot and dry in the third degree and best administered boiled in wine or in a raw egg.

In his book *Health's Improvement*, Thomas Muffet makes a differentiation between the 'tame', cultivated duck and the wild variety. Home-reared young ducklings he considers good to eat. To him, this is evidence that man can change harmful nature and turn it into something wholesome. Wild ducks pose a real danger, in his opinion, because he believes them to only feed on grass, worms, spawns of fish frogs fat mud which makes them 'lecherous'.

By 1599 Henry Butts is not quite as terrified by ducks or mallards but still remains on the cautious side: ducks are hot and moist in the second degree, perfumed at the mouth with borage and suitable for cold weather only. This meat is best for people with strong stomachs who undertake great exercise.

TO ROSTE VENISON

Transcribed original recipe

> Let your Venison be perboyled, then make it tender, and cast into it colde water, then Larde it and roste it, and for sauce: take broth, Vinegar, Pepper, Cloves and Mace, with a little salte, and boyle all these together, and so upon your Venison serve it.

The Good Huswifes Handmaide for the Kitchin, 1594

Modernised recipe

- ◆ Venison joint
- ◆ Bacon slices
- ◆ Chicken stock
- ◆ A little mild apple vinegar
- ◆ Pepper, ground to taste
- ◆ Cloves, mace and salt to taste

Bring your stock to the boil and cook the venison joint for half the time it needs for being cooked. Remove from the stock and hold under cold water. Leave to drain. Wrap bacon slices around it and roast it in the oven or in a rotisserie. In

the meantime, add the spices and vinegar to the broth and allow to cook for roughly the same time as the venison takes to roast. Remove whole mace and cloves. Serve the roast in a serving dish with the sauce around it.

There is an almost identical recipe in the *A Book of Cookry*, 1591.

Additional information

Christmas fell right in the hunting season and so venison was clearly a popular choice for those who had access to game. Most recipes call for boiled or roasted venison and baked in a pie. In Tudor times venison included all wild meats, not just deer as we do now. The act of carving deer was termed as 'breaking'.

Venison was generally not available to purchase but account books often show rewards for bringing a deer, such as an entry for 1569 in the *Dinner Book of the London Drapers' Company*, where 5s were paid to the Lord's Treasurer's servant for one buck brought into the hall.[43] In a letter to Lady Lisle dated 6 July 1534, Richard Norton thanks her for the provision of vension.[44]

Venison was regarded as a 'Lordes dysshe' by Andrew Boorde as well as unsuitable for the hard-working lower class, and the hunting of deer was a right 'princely pastime'.

Successful merchants, yeomen farmers and craftsmen with money to spare did on occasion try to break the rules, and town council members, lord mayors, merchants and master craftsmen by trade would happily receive such gifts.

On 29 August 1559 Henry Machyn observed that venison was included in the Merchant Tailor's feast.[45] In his only surviving letter to his wife, Elizabeth, on 29 November 1525, Thomas Cromwell sends her a deer.[46] Henry VIII's privy purse accounts show several entries for deer being gifted to the king. On 27 February 1530 's'vnt of maister lewkens' got rewarded 10s for bringing a buck.

TO BAKE A RED DEARE

Transcribed original recipe

Take a handful of time, a hand full of rosemarie, a hand full of winter sauorie, a hand full of bay leaues and a hand full of fennel, and when your liquor seeths that you perboyle your venison in, put in your hearbes also and perboyle your venison vntil it be halfe enough, then take it out and lay it vpon a faire boorde that the water may runne out from it, then take a knife and pricke it full of holes, and while it is warme haue a faire traye with vineger therein, and so put your venison therein from morning vntill night, and euer nowe and then turne it vpside downe, and then at night haue your coffin ready, and this done season it with synamome, ginger, and nutmegges, pepper and salte, and when you haue seasoned it, put it into your coffin, and put a good quantitie of sweete butter into it, and then put it into the Ouen at night, when you goe to bedde, and in the morning drawe it forth, and put in a saucer full of vineger into your pye at a hole aboue in the toppe of it, so that the vineger may runne into everie place of it, and then stop the whole againe and turne the bottome vpward and so serve it in.

The Good Husvvifes Iewell, 1596, Thomas Dawson

Modernised recipe

- ◆ Venison fillet (enough for 2 people)
- ◆ ½ a handful of fresh thyme, rosemary, winter savory and bay leaves
- ◆ ½ a handful of fennel seeds
- ◆ Homemade or ready-bought shortcrust pastry
- ◆ ½ cup vinegar (verjuice – mild apple vinegar)
- ◆ Ground cinnamon, ginger, nutmeg, pepper and salt to taste
- ◆ A little butter

For this recipe you need to preboil your meat as it is left whole. Put your meat in a pan and cover it with water. Add your herbs (no need to chop) and allow to cook for about 10 minutes to seal the meat. Remove from the water and allow to drain. Poke with a sharp knife several times. Put meat into a plastic vessel with vinegar and leave overnight (or prepare in the morning and use in the evening) to absorb the flavour.

Rollout your pastry and place the whole fillet into the middle. Save the vinegar for later. Season with the spices and add a few knobs of butter. Wrap the pastry around the meat. Bake very slowly at low medium heat. The longer the better. Mine took 3 hours. Remove from the oven, make a small hole in the top and carefully fill in the vinegar from the dressing. Close the hole and turn the pastry on its top. If the bottom is not completely cooked, return to the oven for a few more minutes until the bottom of the pie is done too. Remove, serve on a nice platter and enjoy!

Additional information

On 1 September 1585 Robert Dudley's disbursement book shows 20s delivered to Battey at Grafton by his lordship's commandment for 'bakyng of red deare pasties' for his lordship at Grafton.[47]

Quite interesting are the numbers of venison pasties gifted to various judges of Assize. In 1596-7 the judges Thomas Walmsley and Edward Fenner, riding the western and Oxford circuits, received at least four venison pasties or baked deer and a red deer-pie on 24 July 1598 at Exeter Castle.[48]

In his book *A Dietary of Helth*, Tudor physician Andrew Boorde is clearly a big fan of venison and calls English deer the best in the whole Christendom. A' lords dyssche' for 'good Englysshe man'. In the *Castel of Helth* Sir Thomas Elyot, tells the reader that the flesh of red deer is far better than the one of fallow deer.

Thomas Muffet dedicates quite a long section on the debate whether deer is the worst or best meat. He finally concludes that all its shortcomings could be easily rectified by a good cook who understands how to prepare it well.

In 1584, Thomas Cogan cannot understand why people are so keen on venison that they would not shy away from stealing it if they cannot otherwise come by it. The only way to eat venison in his opinion is to drown it in wine first.

In 1599 Henry Butts calls red deer exceedingly good nourishment and recommends roasting or baking it in pasties with lots of fat. The flesh is hot in the first and dry in the second degree. He is the only one who claims that the flesh fallow deer is more nourishing than red deer and requires roasting with a lot of oil.

TO BOYLE MUTTON WITH NAUONS (TURNIPS)

Transcribed original recipe

> First pill your Nauons, and wash them then cut fiue or sixe of them into peeces to the bignes of an inche, and when your mutton hath boiled a while take out al the licour sauing so much as may couer well the mutton, then put the Nauons into the pot of mutton with a handful of parselye, chopped fine, and a branche of Rosemary, seasoning it with salt pepper and saffron.

The Second Part of the Good Hus-wiues Iewell, 1597

Modernised recipe

- ◆ Fillet of mutton or lamb
- ◆ 1-2 big turnips, peeled and cubed

- ◆ Handful of fresh parsley, chopped
- ◆ 1 sprig of fresh rosemary
- ◆ Salt, pepper and crushed saffron to taste

Cook your meat in sufficient water in an ovenproof dish (with lid) in the oven at medium heat for about one hour or until done. Use this stock to boil your turnips. Add spices and the rosemary sprig and boil until done. Remove the rosemary, add meat and parsley and serve hot.

Additional information

Nauons or navens was the Tudor name for turnips. Turnips had a much better reputation than parsnips and, unlike the latter, turnips feature relatively often in Tudor recipes.

In 1584 English physician Thomas Cogan said about the turnip that it is hot and moist in temperature and nourishing if first boiled in water and then served in a fat meat broth (such as the one above). According to him, the addition of pepper is necessary to reduce the 'wind'.

TO MAKE MINST PYES

Transcribed original recipe

Take your Veale and perboyle it a little, or mutton, then set it a
cooling: and when it is colde, take three pound of suit to a legge
of mutton, or fower pound to a fillet of Veale, and thē mince them
small by them selues, or together whether you will, then take to
season them halfe an vnce of Nutmegs, half an vnce of cloues
and Mace, halfe an vnce of Sinamon, a little Pepper, as much
Salt as you think will season them, either to the mutton or to the
Veale, take viij. yolkes of Egges when they be hard, half a pinte
of rosewater full measure, halfe a pound of Suger, then straine
the Yolkes with the Rosewater and the Suger and mingle it with
your meate, if ye haue any Orrenges or Lemmans you must take
two of them, and take the pilles very thin and mince them very
smalle, and put them in a pound of currans, six dates, half a pound
of prunes laye Currans and Dates vpon the top of your meate, you
must take two or three Pomewaters or Wardens and mince with

your meate, you maye make them woorsse if you will, if you will make good crust put in three or foure yolkes of egges a litle Rosewater, & a good deale of suger.

The Good Hous-wiues Treasurie, 1588

Modernised recipe

- ◆ Veal or lamb mince (approx. 560-690g)
- ◆ 1 batch of fine pastry (homemade or ready bought)
- ◆ 340g suet (beef fat) for lamb or 450g for veal
- ◆ Approx. 120g currants
- ◆ Approx. 120g prunes (chopped)
- ◆ Approx. 120g candied orange and/or lemon peel (chopped)
- ◆ 1-2 dates (chopped)
- ◆ 1-2 wardens or hard pears (peeled, cored and chopped)
- ◆ Approx. 2.5g ground nutmeg
- ◆ Approx. 2.5g ground mace
- ◆ ½ teaspoon cloves (careful – this spice can numb your mouth)
- ◆ Ground black pepper, to taste
- ◆ 2 egg yolks (hard boiled and chopped)
- ◆ 60ml /¼ cup rosewater (I recommend plain water with a few drops of rosewater as it is very strong and probably much stronger than it once was)
- ◆ 50-60g sugar

This recipe is rather 'modern' in it that it gives fairly specific measurements. However, given that an average leg of a lamb weighs between 2.25kg and 2.75kg (4-6lb) which would easily feed eight or more people, I have quartered all the given amounts to retain the authentic measurements but make it more twenty-first-century appropriate.

Mix all solid ingredients in a bowl. Mix rosewater with egg yolks and sugar and blend. Mix both together and back into your pie pastry. Leave enough pastry for a lid. Leave a funnel (hole) in the middle.

Bake in the oven at medium heat until done which may take as long as 2 hours. In Tudor times mince pies were always big and tall with a fairly self-supporting pie crust. The bite-size mince pie is not something the Tudors would have recognized.

The original recipe instructs the pastry (crust) to be made from 3-4 yolks, a little rosewater and sugar.

Additional information

According to food historian Peter Breas, the association of pies of minced meats with Christmas appears to have developed in the mid-sixteenth century.[49] In 1573 Thomas Tusser confirmed that 'Beef, mutton and pork shred pies of the best' already formed an essential part of 'Christmas Husbandry Fare'.[50]

Christmas pies were often made with shredded leftover meats – mostly mutton – in commemoration of the shepherds. Sugar, dried fruit and spices were then added.

There is also a poem by Robert Herrick (1591-1674) on that subject:

> Come, guard this night the Christmas pie,
> That the thief, though ne'er so sly,
> With his flesh-hooks don't come nigh
> To catch it.
> From him who all alone sits there,
> Having his eyes still in his ear,
> And deal of nightly fear,
> To watch it.

TO MAK CABAGE WORTIS

Transcribed original recipe text

> To mak cabages wortis tak whit cabage and shred them smale and mak them up, also tak whit cabages and cut them from the stalks and wesche them and parboile them and presse out the water and hew them smale in flesche tym put fat brothe of beef in a pot of capon brothe or the brothe of other good flesche and when it is boiled put in thy cabages and maribones all to broken and boile them up do ther to saffron or salt and alay it upe with grond bred and luk it be chargant of canebyns and serue it.

A Noble Book off Cookry ffor a Prynce Houssolde, c.1480-1500

Modernised recipe

- ◆ 1 head of pale cabbage
- ◆ Beef stock – approx. 1l
- ◆ Chicken stock – approx. ½ l

- ◆ 1 bone marrow
- ◆ 2-3 strands of crushed saffron
- ◆ Salt to taste
- ◆ Some fresh breadcrumbs
- ◆ Some cooked, shelled and mashed fava beans to thicken liquid

Remove stalk from cabbage and shred the rest into bite-size chunks. Boil them in water until almost soft, remove from water and allow them to drain. Boil up the beef stock and add the chicken stock. Allow to boil and add bone marrow and cabbage. Cook until cabbage is soft, then add saffron and salt. Much of the stock will now have evaporated – add breadcrumbs, some mashed fava beans and stir -allow to boil a little longer on low heat to thicken the sauce. Serve hot.

Additional information

This recipe is written in Middle English. *Chargant* means thickening and *canebyns* refer to beans made in a certain way. This recipe for cabbage dates to the reign of Henry VII and is typical for the use during the winter months, when few other green vegetables would grow. The use of beef and chicken stock (broth) make it only suitable for 'flesh days' such as Mondays, Tuesdays,

Thursdays and Sundays. On Wednesday, Friday or Saturday the meat broth would have to be substituted with a fish broth.

Before 1550 there was little interest in vegetables among the nobility in Tudor England and cabbage was no exception. It is therefore rather surprising to see such a recipe entirely focusing on the preparation of cabbage, a low-status vegetable, without meat. Cabbages were either grown in the kitchen garden from purchased seeds or fresh from markets or neighbouring estates which had a surplus.

In the Middle Ages there were two kinds of cabbages available in England, the headless kale or colewort and the headed variety which was more popular on the Continent. In 1587 William Harrison states in *The Description of England* that in his time cabbage is no longer food of the poor but features also as dainty dishes at the tables of delicate merchants, gentlemen and the nobility.[51]

Tudor physician Andrew Boorde, whose readership was the affluent class, does not even mention cabbage in *A Dyetary of Helth*, published in 1542. Sir Thomas Elyot in his book *The Castel of Helth*, is not taken by cabbage as food but recognizes its place as medicine. He states that some eat the leaves raw with vinegar before meat and he suggests also that this is good against drunkenness.

In 1584 Thomas Cogan more or less repeats what has already being said but he adds that colewort and cabbage are hot and dry in the first degree and boiled are good with beef, vinegar and pepper. Thomas Muffet explains that there are diverse sorts of coleworts and mentions that the best ones are white-leafed 'cauliflores' so beloved by the Italians.

In 1599 Henry Butts gives instructions on how to prepare cabbages for best results: seething them in water first, then in a fat flesh broth with pepper. Best enjoyed in the prime of spring.

FRIED MEAT OF TURNEPS

Translated, original recipe

> Rost the Turnops in the embers, or else séeth them whole, then cut or slice them in péeces as thicke as halfe the haft of a knife, which done, take cheese and cut it in the same form and quantity, but some what thinner, then take Sugar, Pepper, and other spices mingled together, and put them in a pan vnder the péeces of cheese, as if you would make a crust vnder the cheese, and on the top of them likewise, and ouer it you shall lay the péeces of Turneps, couering them ouer with the spices aforesaid, and

plenty of good Butter, and so you shall doe with the said cheese and Turneps till the pan bée full, letting them fry the space of a quarter of an houre, or more, like a Tart, and this would be one of your last dishes.

Epulario, 1598 English translation

Modernised recipe

- ◆ 1 medium sized turnip per person
- ◆ Approx. 250g cheese, preferably Italian such as mozzarella
- ◆ Approx. 2 tbsp of unsalted butter
- ◆ Seasoning to taste: sugar and pepper as stated and others such as cinnamon, ginger, nutmeg or mace

Roast turnips in foil in the oven until soft. Remove from the oven, allow to cool and slice into finger-thick pieces, cutting off the very top and bottom. Cut your cheese in slightly thinner strips. Mix all the spices and sprinkle into a pie pan. Cover with a layer of cheese followed by a layer of turnips. Add more spices and a few knobs of butter. Add the last layer of cheese and bake in the oven at medium heat until the cheese turns golden brown. Serve hot!

The Italian author of this recipe suggests serving this dish towards the end of dinner. This recipe has a very Italian feel to it as the English hardly ever use cheese in their cooking like this.

Additional information

Rector William Harrison, author of *Food and Drink of the English* (1587), affirms those dates by commenting that turnips had been growing and haven been eaten in plenty in the late-thirteenth and early-fourteenth centuries but were then neglected until the beginning of the sixteenth century around 1510.

Physician Sir Thomas Elyot expressed a strong view in favour of turnip in his book *Castel of Helth* from 1539, but in 1548 William Forrest had declared that 'our English nature cannot live by roots'.

Turnips were often described by physicians as hot and moist, flatulent and to be an aphrodisiac. According to English herbalist John Gerard, turnips were eaten mostly boiled and roasted but sometimes raw (Wales). He mentions also that occasionally they were used as boiled salads.[52]

FRUMENTE

Transcribed original recipe

> To mak furmente tak whet and pik it clene and put it in a mortair and bray it till it hull then wenowe it and wesshe it nd put it unto the pot and boile it till it brest then fett it down and play it up with cow mylk till yt be enough alay it with yolks of eggs and kep it that it byrn not, colour it with saffron do ther to sugar and salt it and serue it.

A Noble Book off Cookry ffor a Prynce Houssolde, c.1480-1500

Modernised recipe

- ◆ 1 handful of pearl barley per person (cuts out the crushing of the wheat)
- ◆ Enough stock to cover the pearl barley in your pot
- ◆ 2 egg yolks
- ◆ Salt and sugar to taste
- ◆ 1-2 strands of crushed saffron
- ◆ A cup of milk

Heat up stock, add the pearl barley and the saffron, let it boil on low heat until the pearl barley is thickening up. Take it off the heat and let it soak for some time. Check the consistency. If still too hard, add more stock and allow to boil a little longer. When soft, remove from the heat, add salt and egg yolks plus the milk (or almond milk). Do not allow the mixture to boil once the eggs have been added. Keep warm until being served. If you wish, decorate with dried rose petals, cornflower or crystalised violet or rose petals.

Additional information

Frumenty is a wheat-based dish which has been traditionally served alongside meat at Christmas for centuries. It is delicious and easy to prepare. The dish takes its name from *frumentum*, the Latin word for corn, and there are many variations and slightly different spellings of the name.

Frumenty was a Christmas staple for much of the nation. There are regional varied recipes, but most consisted of cracked wheat which was boiled into a thick porridge and improved with the addition of milk, almond milk, eggs or cream. In wealthier households, spices such as saffron, cinnamon or mace would also have been used. People of lower status would have eaten frumenty on its own, but in wealthier households it was often served to accompany venison or mutton. Any grains could be used and lightly cracked in a pestle and mortar.

English physician Andrew Boorde said about frumente in 1542: 'Fyrmente is made of whete and mylke, in the whiche, yf flesshe be sodden, to eate it is not commendable, for it is harde of dygestyon; but whan it is digested it doth nourysshe, and it doth strength a man'.

In 1584 Thomas Cogan states that wheat is not only used in bread but 'being sodden it is used for meat (meal), as I have seene in sundry places & of some is used to be buttered'. He goes on to say that Galen himself was offered this dish when he visited somebody in the country but concluded that it was heavy and hard to digest and better suited for labouring people.

One of the oldest English frumenty recipes appears in *A Forme of Cury* from c.1390.

EISANDS WITH OTEMEALE GROTES

Transcribed original recipe text

> Take a pinte of Creame and seethe it, and when it is hot, put therto
> a pinte of Otemeale grotes, and let them soke in it all night, and

put therto viii. Yolks of egs, and a little Pepper, Cloves, mace, and saffron, and a good deale of Suet of beefe, and small Raisins and Dates, and a little Sugar.

A book of Cookrye, 1591, A.W

Modernised recipe

- ½ pint (approx. 1 cup) of fresh cream
- Same amount oatmeal
- 4 egg yolks
- A little ground pepper, cloves, mace and crushed saffron to taste
- 2-3tbsp lard (beef fat)
- Small handful of raisins and chopped dates
- A little sugar to taste

Heat up the cream and stir in the spices, the melted fat and the oatmeal. Leave to stand overnight. Gently reheat before use the next day and if necessary, add a little milk if too stiff. Add sugar, egg yolks, raisins and dates and serve hot.

Additional information

This dish is very similar to frumente (see above), another very popular dish that often accompanied venison or game dishes. This variety has the added cream, which makes it very much richer and therefore I have roughly halved the quantities. You can substitute the cream with a plant alternative and omit the egg yolks.

This dish is also sometimes referred to as 'gruel'. Andrew Boorde says about it in *A Dyetary of Helth*: 'Sewe and stewpottes, and *grewell* made with otmell, in all the which no herbes be put in, can do lytel displeasure except that it doth replete a man with ventosyte; but it relaxeth the belly.'

In *The Haven of Heath*, Thomas Cogan observes, that in Lancashire he has seen people make a meal from oats who refer to it as 'greats or groats'. For this meal they use dried oats boiled in water with salt. The same boiled in whey is called whey-pottage and made with ale, ale-pottage. In his opinion this makes a wholesome and temperate meal for a light digestion and he must have liked it so much that he advises everyone to try it.

A FIGGE

Transcribed original recipe text

> To mak a figge tak figges and boile them in wyne then bray them
> in a mortair put ther to bred and boile it with wyne cast ther to
> clowes maces guinger pynes and hole raissins and florishe it with
> pongarnettes and serue it.

A Noble Boke off Cookry ffor a Prynce Houssolde, c.1480-1500

Modernised recipe

- ◆ Dried figs (I used 6)
- ◆ Approx. 500ml sweet wine
- ◆ Handful of fresh breadcrumbs
- ◆ Ground cloves, ground mace, ground ginger to taste
- ◆ Handful of pine kernels
- ◆ Handful of raisins
- ◆ Pomegranate kernels for decoration

Boil the figs in wine until soft. Add breadcrumbs and mash mixture with hand blender. Add spices, pine kernels and raisins. Put mixture into a serving dish and sprinkle pomegranate kernels on top. Serve hot or cold.

Figge is the ancestor of boiled plum pudding and Christmas pudding. Fygey pudding was originally served on Palm Sunday but became a popular dish at Christmas too. This would have been a very expensive dish at the time of Henry VII. Except for the breadcrumbs, all ingredients had to be imported, making it only affordable for the affluent class.

Additional information

Pomegranates were very popular early in the Tudor period. The seeds were used for decoration and the juice in sauces and chicken dishes.

Robert Dudley, Earl of Leicester, purchased high-value foods frequently. The household books of his accountant William Chancy between 1558-9 show a purchase of pomegranates for 2s.[53]

Expensive food gifts were always deemed most suitable for the monarch. On 16 January 1531 Sampson's servant was rewarded 10s for bringing pomegranates to the king's grace.[54]

Tudor diet writers and physicians had only good things to say about this fruit. Andrew Boorde called it 'nutrytyue and good for the stomacke'. In his book *Health's improvement* Thomas Muffet praises the sweet pomegranate as a cure for a number of ailments and recommends that this fruit is best in winter especially for old men. In 1599 Henry Butts classifies the sweet pomegranates as temperately hot and moist and the sour type colder. He recommends the sweet variety for use in winter and the sour for summer, especially the young.

A TARTE TO PROVOKE COURAGE EITHER IN MAN OR WOMAN

Transcribed original recipe

> A Tarte to provoke courage either in Man or Woman. Take a quart of good wine, and boyle therin two Burre rootes scrapped cleane, two good Quinces, and a Potation roote well pared and an ounce of Dates, and when all these are boyled verie tender, let them be drawne through a strainer wine and al, and then put in the yolks of eight Egs, and the braines of three or foure cocke Sparrowes, and straine them into the other, and a little Rosewater, and seeth them

all with Sugar, Synamon and Ginger, and cloves and Mace, and
put in a little Sweet Butter, and set it upon a chafingdish of coals
between two platters, and so let it boyle till it be something big.

The Good Huswifes Handmaide for the Kitchin, 1594

Modernised recipe

- ◆ Enough white wine to cover fruit and sweet potato in pot
- ◆ 1tbsp dried, chopped burrow root (obtainable from health shop)
- ◆ 1-2 peeled, cored and chopped quinces
- ◆ 1 peeled and chopped sweet potato
- ◆ Approx. 1oz/25g chopped dried dates
- ◆ 4-6 egg yolks
- ◆ A few drops of rosewater (to your taste)
- ◆ Sugar, ground cinnamon, ground ginger, ground cloves and ground
  mace to your taste
- ◆ 1tbsp unsalted butter
- ◆ Pastry cases
- ◆ The sparrow brains may be substituted for a tbsp bone marrow or
  left out altogether.

Boil the quince, sweet potato, dates and burrow root in the wine until soft. Allow to cool slightly, mash with hand blender, add yolks and all other remaining ingredients. Return to pot and cook on low heat for a few more minutes. Spoon mixture into pastry cases and serve hot or cold.

Additional information

This recipe is the first one, together with an identical one from Thomas Dawson's *The Good Housewife's Jewell* from 1596/7, which features sweet potatoes. Together with the turkey, the sweet potato, a vine from the morning glory family, was an instant success with the English after it was first encountered on Hispaniola where it was introduced by the Spanish from Panama in 1508.

Within eight years it had reached Spain, but it took a few more decades to reach England. The Spanish potato, as it was also known, was also valued for its supposedly aphrodisiac powers much praised and desired by Shakespeare's Sir John Falstaff in *The Merry Wives of Windsor* when he wishes for 'the sky to rain potatoes'.

Polite European sixteenth-century society classified the sweet potato as 'rich man's food' being rare, expensive and not easy to grow in England's climate. John Hawkins, an English mariner and slave trader, summed it up as the most delicate root that may be eaten.

In 1597 John Gerard elevated it even further by holding the sweet potato plant in his portrait on the front of his 'Herbal'. In his entry, he mildly bemoans the fact that his plant failed to produce a flower and did not make it through the winter. He also makes a clear distinction between the sweet potato and the Virginian potato, better known as the common potato, which took another 200 years to find its way into the English kitchen. The sweet potato was recommended by Gerard for the use in confectionaries, but he states also that the roots can be roasted in the ashes, then infused in wine and dressed in oil, vinegar and salt. In his opinion, they comfort, nourish and strengthen the body as well as producing bodily lust. A big thumb's up for a vegetable.

The sweet potato was not being discussed in any of the books written by dietary writers or physicians in Tudor England. The herbalist John Gerard remains our only English source from the sixteenth century.

TO MAKE A DYSCHEFULL OF SNOWE

Transcribed original recipe

> Take a pottell of swete thycke creame and the whytes of eyghte egges, and beate them together wyth a spone, then putte them in

youre creame and a saucerfull of Rosewater, and a dyshe full of
Suger wyth all, then take a styke and make it cleane, and than cutte
it in the ende foure square, and therwith beate all the aforesayde
thynges together, and ever as it ryseth take it of and put it into a
Collaunder, this done take one apple and set it in the myddes of
it, and a thicke bush of Rosemary, and set it in the myddes of the
platter, then cast your Snowe upon the Rosemarye, and fyll your

platter therwith. And yf you have wafers caste some in wyth all and thus seve them forthe.

A Proper Newe Booke of Cokerye, c.1557

Modernised recipe

- ◆ Whites from 4 large eggs
- ◆ Cup of very fine sugar (icing/powder sugar)
- ◆ Rosewater to your taste (as it is very strong)
- ◆ Approx. 100ml double cream
- ◆ Small sprigs of rosemary
- ◆ 1 apple, peeled and cored
- ◆ Tudor wafers or ratafia/amaretti biscuits

Beat the egg white with a hand mixer until it turns thick enough that it won't fall out of your jug when slightly tipping it. (Make sure that there is absolutely no egg yolk or grease in the bowl before you begin as this would prevent the egg white from forming a snow) Add sugar carefully. Whip the cream in a food mixer and add to the stiffened egg whites. Place the apple in the middle. Tip the rosemary sprig in the 'snow' and place into the middle of the apple. Spoon the remaining 'snow' around the apple making it look like a tree on a hill in a wintery landscape. Sprinkle wafers or biscuits on top. I used strawberries for decoration, but that is not part of the recipe.

Additional information

This dish was very popular across Europe and is one of the first recipes to describe the process of beating the egg white into 'snow'. The instructions of the recipe are not all that clear, but it is pretty obvious that the egg whites were beaten before the other ingredients were mixed in. This was a revelation and until this point it had not been done. To create little air pockets inside the beaten egg whites would help to improve the quality of cake-making in time to come.

The Tudors were not too fond of egg whites and considered this part of the egg not very healthy. Egg white was primely used for clarifying sugar and any broth where a clear fluid was desired. Most Tudor physicians gave egg white a 'cold' quality and Andrew Boorde even called it 'viscus'. Henry Butts the Elizabethan physician, backs Boorde's 'cold' attribution for egg white in his 'table talk' section of his publication in 1599: 'The white is cold, the yolke is hot'.

TO MAKE A (TWELFTH) CAKE

Transcribed original recipe

Take a peck of flower, and fower pound of currance, one ounce
of Cinamon, half an ounce of ginger, two nutmegs, of cloves and
mace two pennyworth, of butter one pound, mingle your spice and
flower & fruit together, put as much barme as will make it light,
then take good Ale & put your butter in it, all saving a little, which
you must put in the milk, & let the milk boyle with the butter, then
make a posset withy it & temper the Cake with the posset drink &
curd & all together, & put some sugar in & so bake it.

Elinor Fettiplace's Receipt Book, 1647

Modernised recipe

- ◆ 730g flour
- ◆ 225g currants
- ◆ Ground cinnamon, ginger, nutmeg and mace to taste
- ◆ A very little ground cloves (makes your mouth go numb)
- ◆ 220ml milk
- ◆ 220ml ale
- ◆ 50g butter
- ◆ A little sugar, to taste
- ◆ 25g fresh yeast or 10g dried yeast

Mix the flour with the currants and the spices. Prepare your 'posset' by gently warming the milk up to body temperature in a pot. Add the ale, butter and a little sugar. Dissolve the yeast in a little of this posset. Add the yeast mixture to the flour mixture and knead until it feels like a bread mixture. You may need to add more milk or flour as you go. The right texture is more important than precise measurements. When the right texture is achieved, place the dough into a bowl, cover with a cloth and leave it somewhere warm to rise for about an hour or so. You know that it has risen enough when it has doubled its size. Knead the dough again and place it into a greased loaf tin. Allow it to rest and rise again in a warm place, covered up with a cloth. This might take between 30 and 40 minutes. Bake in the preheated oven at medium heat until it is baked. This might take 2-3 hours. Check with a baking skewer – if it comes out clean when poking the cake, you know it is ready.

The original quantities were given that the original recipe was catering for a huge household. The recipe here, as worked out by Hilary Spurling, shows reduced measurements.

Additional information

A peck is the fourth of a bushel, or 12½lb. Yeast was the only raising agent known to the Tudors.

Sir William Petre of Ingatestone Hall in Essex entertained his Twelfthtide guests on 6 January 1552 with this specially baked, spicy fruit cake containing a bean and a pea for the King and Queen of the Revels. Shakespeare's *Twelfth Night* was written for this sort of seasonal party – three years before Elinor wrote her recipe book. By the seventeenth century, Samuel Pepys had his own Twelfth Night cake which cost him 20s and it was cut into twenty slices.[56]

Sadly, there is no surviving original recipe from the Tudor period for this truly delicious Christmas-themed cake. There are original recipes for similar 'fine cake' but without the dried fruit and the Twelve Night themed bean and pea.

LAMB'S WOOL FOR WASSAILING

Lamb's wool is a warm spiced drink and has been used for wassailing for hundreds of years, using either mulled ale or cider. Sadly, no contemporary recipe appears to have survived.

Modern interpretation of traditional Elizabethan Lamb's Wool hot drink

- ◆ Ale or cider
- ◆ Peeled and diced apples
- ◆ Brown sugar to taste
- ◆ Ground cinnamon, ginger and nutmeg to taste
- ◆ Some slices of toasted bread for the wassailing – optional

Roast the apples until the pieces turn soft and heat the ale/cider in a pot. Add sugar and spices. Stir and simmer for a few minutes. Add apples and serve hot next to your apple tree, should you have one!

For the sheer fun of it, dunk your toasted bread in the lamb's wool and hang it up on your tree and enjoy Tudor traditions! Wassail!

Additional information

A wassail bowl (see picture) full of spiced cider or lamb's wool was carried out to the orchard. The ancient custom of wassailing took place in the orchard. All the participants gathered around the oldest tree, and a piece of toast would be dipped in the wassail bowl and placed either on the roots or in the branches of the tree to attract good spirits. One of several possible wassail songs would be sung, sometimes several times as the crowd got into the swing of things. Then, the lamb's wool in the wassail bowl would be poured over the roots of the tree, and the men would return to the house for more fun and merrymaking.

In Kent in 1585 wassailing was being done by the teenage men of the villages. By the 1590s, if not much earlier, bowls of hot, spiced ale mixed with roasted crab apples were being served as 'lamb's wool', a name suggestive of its warm, soft and comforting nature. There is a debate as to the origin of the name, but when the pulp of baked apple is added to the drink it thickens the brew and looks like lamb's wool. However, it may be derived from the Irish Gaelic *la mas nbhal* pronounced *lamass-ool*, made for the feast of apple gathering known as All Hallows Eve or Lammastide. Each guest would take a piece of apple and eat it, toasting his/her fellows.

The custom of wassailing was first described by Peter de Langtoft in the 1320s, where a leader of a gathering cried 'wassail' (old English for 'your health'). The famous eighth-century poem *Beowulf* mentions wassail as a toast (Anglo Saxon for 'be of good health'). Its use with drink was recorded by Geoffrey of Monmouth and by Wace in his Roman de Brut.[56]

From a toast, wassail came to refer to the practice of drinking in revelry for wassail at Christmas and to the drink itself.

In more rustic establishments the drink was served in a milking pail, as described in John Bale's play *Kynge John*, from around 1550:

> Wassayle, wassayle out of the milking payle
> Wassayle, wassayle, as white as my nayle
> Wassayle, wassayle, in snow, frost and hayle ...
> Wassayle, wassayle, that never will fayle[57]

Most households had a wooden wassail bowl which contained the hot, spiced drink and a bite-size chunk of bread (cake) at the bottom. People would pass the bowl crying 'wassail' and each recipient would take a drink and pass it on, saying 'drinkhail'. The bread at the bottom was reserved for the most important person in the room, the origin of the later custom of 'toasting' at celebrations.

Children would sometimes carry the wassail bowl from house to house to be shared and replenished, as Thomas Kirchmaier (1571-63) describes:

> There cities are where boys and girls together still do run
> About the streets with like as soon as night begins to come,
> And bring abroad their wassail- bowls, who well rewarded be
> With cakes, and cheese, and great good cheer, and money plenteously[58]

On Twelfth Eve in 1555 an especially flamboyant version of the custom was experienced by the Londoner Henry Machyn when he attended a party at Henley on Thames as a guest. He reports: 'ther cam a xij wessells, with maydens syngyng with ther wessells, and after cam the cheyff wyffies syngyng with ther wessells; and the gentyll-woman had hordenyd a grett tabull of bankett, dyssys of spyssus and frut, as marmelad, gynbred, gele, comfett, suger plat, and dyver odur,'[59]

In his book 'Herball', John Gerard said in 1597 that 'the flesh of the pomewater apple cooked with water and wine is a drink known as Lambes Wooll'. Apparently drunk at night within one hour makes you go to the toilet.[60]

On Twelfth Night (6 January) farmers would wassail their trees by pouring the drink over the roots to ensure a bountiful harvest. The practice survives even today, but it is also mentioned by Robert Herrick (1648):

> Wassail the trees, that they may bear
> You many plum and many a pear:
> For more or less fruits they will bring,
> As you do give them wassailing.

Twelfth Night was celebrated with great ceremony in royal and noble households and each person was served their own wassail cake and cup of wassail drink. The chapel choir sang in the wassail, followed by carols.

Shakespeare's *Midsummer Night's Dream* confirms that crab apples in lamb's wool were left whole, rather than beaten in as a pulp:

> Sometimes I lurk in gossip's bowl
> In very likeness of a roasted crab,

And when she drinks, against her lips I bob,
And down her withered dewlap pours the ale
Or when,
… Marion's nose looks red and raw,
When roasted crabs hiss in the bowl
The nightly sgs the staring owl,
To-whit!

Chapter 5

BANQUETING FOOD

Banqueting Food in Tudor Times

The banquet is a distinctively Tudor social institution that began at the highest level at court and soon filtered down as a new fashion for all well-to-do families in England. Its popularity was aided by the increased quantity of sugar that became available in England and the introduction of the banqueting house – a place specifically designed for eating portable banqueting food in a pleasant but private surrounding.

Unlike today, the banquet in Tudor times generally referred to the last part of a feast, which was more or less the dessert course, and attendance was by special invitation only. During the feast, diners were seated according to their position, rank or standing in society, but the banquet that followed offered a much more exciting prospect of free choice in where to sit and of your conversation partner!

The term banquet derives from the Italian word *banchetto* for small side table or bench on which the food was served. It first appeared in print in its plural form as *bankettis* in Caxton's edition of the *Golden Legend*, published in 1483.[1]

During Henry VII's reign the feast incorporated sweet and savoury dishes side by side and the end of such a feast was signalled by the arrival of the so-called *void* when the trestle tables were first cleared and then put away. During the *void* the diners enjoyed a drink of hippocras, a spiced wine, and wafers or sugared spices, whilst standing up.

By the 1540s things started to change, and by the 1550s chronicler Hall uses the word 'banquet' as a synonym for the older French term *void*. By the second half of the sixteenth century, with the increasing availability of sugar and the growing range of sweet foodstuffs available, the banquet became all the rage.

In Henry VIII's time the dessert course or banquet started to move away from the feasting held in the Great Hall to a warmer and more private place in the house.

During the reign of Elizabeth I many banqueting rooms moved to a rooftop venue such as seen at Hardwick Hall (1590-97) and Lacock Abbey (1540-1553).

The chief purpose of the banquet was to impress with lavish dramatic displays and a show of the host's wealth, but it also promoted beauty and sex. And what better way to impress foreign ambassadors, as Cromwell did by giving daily banquets in honour of the Scottish ambassador who stayed for New Year 1534.[2] The banquet appealed also because it provided privacy, away from the prying eyes and ears of servants – very much the Tudor clubbing style. The food was served on a side table from which people helped themselves.

The most costly and rarest of foods such as expensive spices, imported dried fruits, sugar, and even food markers like sturgeon were served at the banquet, as one entry from the account of Richard Ellis from 1559-61 for Robert Dudley shows where 11s were paid for one 'vyrkin of sturgeon' was provided for the banquet at Kew.[3]

The cost of the spices and other ingredients for a banquet could easily exceed the cost of labour. Banqueting food was made by skilled artisans – the confectioners – and, of course, at Hampton Court there was a confectionery which produced dishes especially for Henry VIII.

During the late sixteenth century banquet items were prepared sometimes by the lady of the house as the use of confections spread down the social scale. For those who had neither the time or skill some items could be purchased from specialty shops, as the accounts of the Willoughby and Middelton family show us.

In 1577 William Harrison expressed horror at outlandish feasts popular in merchants' households which included 'jellies of all colours, mixed with a variety in the representation of sundry flowers, herbs, trees, forms of beasts, fish, fowls, and fruits, and thereunto marchpane wrought with no small curiosity, tarts of divers hues, and sundry denominations, conserves of old fruits, foreign and home-bred, suckets, codinacs, marmalades, marchpane, sugar bread, gingerbread, Florentines and sundry outlandish confections.'[4]

In 1560 the Skinners' Company held a banquet which Henry Machin describes in his diary as having spiced bread, cherries, strawberries, pippins, marmalade, sucket, comfits, and portyngalles (semi sweet oranges from Portugal), hippocras, claret, and Rhenish wine being offered. [5]

Swiss physician and traveller Thomas Platter described all the lavish banqueting stuff served to him when he joined the Mayor of London in October 1599. Interesting here is to note that it was not just the gentry that enjoyed these sweet luxuries but also middle-ranking civic office holders and guests.

Most banquets included *subtleties* and *sweetmeats*. *Subtleties* are table ornaments and vessels made from sugar paste and served between courses of a feast. This sugar paste (sugar plate) was a made from finely ground sugar, gum dragon, egg white and a liquid – usually rose water. This paste dried hard

and white and was often painted. The most elaborate, costly and impressive banquets and subtleties were served at important state entertainments.

Marchpane was the forefather of marzipan, a confection made from sugar and ground almonds, often baked on a base of wafers and glazed with rosewater and sugar. Marchpane was often used for the creation of subtleties and showpieces at a banquet such as buildings, chess boards or table statues. Elizabeth's master cook, George Webster, made her a chessboard made from marchpane.[6]

Sweetmeats is the collective term for a variety of banqueting food made from sugar, seeds and fruit. Kissing comfits or muscadines and rose sugar were all made of pure sugar and then cut into squares. Wet suckets were various fruits preserved in sugar syrup and served with a two-pronged sucket fork and a small spoon at the other end. Indeed, one of the most popular wet sucket dish, pears in wine, is still popular today. Dry suckets were fruit prepared in sugar syrup then dried before being boxed up, such as candied fruit (fruit peels – orange, lemon), fruit pastes (made from plums, raspberries, pears, apples, lemons, gooseberries, apricots) and the so-called marmalade, a stiff paste like fruit leather, made from quince or oranges, towards the end of the sixteenth century. The first printed recipe for marmalade appeared in 1562 in the book *Secrets* by Alexis of Piedmont. By 1495 imported Portuguese marmalade attracted import duty.

The Tudor notion that fruit was full of water and could therefore cause a harmful imbalance in the body (cold and wet) was helped by the correction of cooking and drying the fruit as seen in banqueting sweetmeat.

Red and white gingerbread was quite different from what we understand by that term today. Tudor gingerbread was made with stale white breadcrumbs ginger, honey, liquorice, anise and red wine. Earlier gingerbreads contained pepper instead of ginger. White gingerbread was made from marzipan, aqua vita and ginger, then moulded, dried and frequently gilded.

Biskets is the collective term for all double-cooked Elizabethan biscuits such as jumbals and cracknels.

Fruit tarts and pies were always popular, and the filling made from strawberries, plum, apple and quince.

Stiff jellies were prepared from sugar and the fruit's natural pectin. Jelly (gele, gelye) was a medieval savoury dish made from fish and meat stock, but by the late sixteenth century it was part of a banquet. Leach (*leche*) was a type of jelly made from rosewater-flavoured milk and thickened with isinglass gelatin made from fish swim bladders. It was then cut into small squares and decorated with gold leaf. These leach jellies were stiff enough to be picked up with fingers.

Tudor cakes and sweet breads were rather dense as the only known rising agent was yeast. Sometimes these sweet breads contained spices and dried fruit such as the Twelfth cake. In 1577 Holinshed referred to sugar bread as one of many 'outlandish' confections indulged in by the gentry.

Wafers were part of the original *voider*, the closing part of a feast in the medieval period. and were made from batter and sometimes rolled up but more commonly made with wafer irons. Wafers were always served with spiced wine known as Hippocras and comfits.

Comfits is the collective term for all sugar-coated seeds, spices or nuts (fennel, anise, coriander, caraway). The word *comfits* derives from the Italian *confetti* and dates to the 1330s. These sugar-coated seeds were occasionally coloured red, yellow or green. Comfits were known by that name in England by the 1480s, and from the 1550s they were fairly common in London. Comfit makers appeared in the 1570s to 1590s and they were usually 'aliens' from Spain, France and Holland. The most successful one was Balthaser Sans (Sanchez) who came to England from Spain in 1547 and was married to an Englishwoman. He supplied marchpanes and other comfits to the London Draper's Company from 1565-78. Norwich admitted its first comfit maker, Isaac Grandage, as a freeman in 1604 and its first sugar maker, Nicholas Reading, was recorded in 1573. The first use of the word 'comfitmaker' is given by the Oxford English Dictionary in 1594 citing Hugh Plat.

Sweetmeats and comfits were also well received and highly regarded food gifts. Gift exchanges between Lord Edward Stanley and Master of the Horse Robert Dudley included comfits. Robert Dudley's account reveal such self-indulgence long before he was granted an earldom by Elizabeth and he owned a small container specifically made for keeping comfits at least after 1579.

In 1562 Queen Elizabeth's 'Svrveiour of the workes' gave her a marchpane bearing the model of St Paul's Cathedral, and Robert Hickes, Yeoman of the Chamber, gave her a marchpane made tower complete with men and artillery.[7]

Thomas Dawson, in *The Good Huswifes Iewell*, provided a list of the names of all things necessary for a banquet, listing amongst other items sugar, pepper, saffron, rosewater, lemons, rice flour and sweet oranges.

Sweet delights and high-value food gifts were also used for bribery and to keep influential people 'sweet'. High-value food like banqueting stuff played a significant political role in the form of food gifts and authorities tried to control and regulate excess consumption through the means of sumptuary laws.

A most iconic product of these banquets was the arrival of trenchers or roundels – round, flat, wooden discs made from sycamore which started to become very trendy in the late 1500s. Their back was painted with a motto, poem, satirical verse, proverbs or moralizing stories. After eating treats from trenchers, they were then turned over and everybody around the table got to read the words on the back. The custom of reading out a joke, riddle or poem such as in our contemporary Christmas crackers is no new thing. These roundels were popular gifts and came in sets of 10,12 or 24.

Trenchers could also be made from sugar paste, gingerbread or marchpane and then eaten.

Elizabethan trenchers (from the author's collection)

The enormous popularity and rise of banqueting food was mostly built on the increased availability of sugar in the sixteenth century. During the early Medieval age, when sugar was rare and expensive, its primary purpose was in medicine and it was reserved for the nobility. It was valued for its 'warming' properties – something always attractive in England.

Sugar's remarkable powers as a preservative became more widely known during the Renaissance. In cookery it was used as a garnish and sprinkled on food. Before the sixteenth century, honey had been the common sweetener, serving to preserve fruits during winter.

Sugar remained an 'affordable' expensive luxury in Tudor England, but with the gradual reduction in cost it began to replace honey as a preservative. A pound of sugar could be bought for between 3d and 4d in the early 1500s, but it fluctuated widely and was always checked by royal proclamation. In 1524 7d was spent on buying sugar in Cambridge for Kenninghall Palace, the Duke of Norfolk's home.[8]

It comes as no surprise that sugar was also used for buying a favour, as the example from Wymondham in Norfolk shows. In 1588/9 'my lorde juge' received one pownd of suger' which had been charged to the town.[9]

In London, the opinion was that sugar was healthier than honey, and with decreasing sugar prices the banquet course came into prominence. The account of William Chancy from 1558-9 for Robert Dudley shows a reward of 3s 4d for Sir John's York's man for bringing a sugar 'lofe'.[10]

Despite sugar's popularity, dietary authors were generally hostile to what they considered the grossly extravagant and unruly banqueting habits of the courtiers. Thomas Muffet states that sweetmeat is of ideal temperate heat and delights the stomach and the liver, fattens the body and gets digested easily. However, he warns of over-sweet and 'gluttish' consumption. Andrew Boorde, however, disagrees. He has no concerns about anything tasting sweet. His contemporary, Sir Thomas Elyot, states that sugar was not mentioned by the ancient authors, but it is 'nowe in dayely experience' is very temperate and nourishing. He also states that sugar can replace honey.

The Elizabethan physician Thomas Cogan explains that sugar is made from sugar cane which grows on the islands of Madeira, Sicily, Cyprus and Rhodes and is suitable for all ages and complexions. He believes sugar is more wholesome than honey but not as hot, and explains that sugar is either brown or white. In 1599 Henry Butts recommends eating sugar with pomegranates and sour oranges. He advises that it is suitable for the winter in cold weather and for old people. He classifies sugar as hot and moist in the first degree.

'Sir Henry Unton's Wedding Feast' at the National Portrait Gallery is probably one of the most iconic paintings illustrating the sheer opulence of a Tudor banquet.

Recipes

TO MAKE IOMBILS A HUNDRED

Transcribed original recipe

> Take twenty Egges and put them into a pot both the yolkes & the white, beat them wel, then take a pound of beaten suger and put to them, and stirre them wel together, then put to it a quarter of a peck of flower, and make a hard paste thereof, and then with Anniseede moulde it well, and make it in little rowles beeing long, and tye them in knots, and wet the ends in Rosewater, then put them into a pan of seething water, but euen in one waum, then take them out with a Skimmer and lay them in a cloth to drie, this being doon lay them in a tart panne, the bottome béeing oyled,

then put them into a temperat Ouen for one howre, turning then often in the Ouen.

The Second Part of the Good Hus-wiues Iewell, 1597, Thomas Dawson

Modern take

- 1 egg per person (whisked)
- Approx. 20-25g sugar per egg (powder or icing sugar if possible)
- Approx. 470-500g flour
- Aniseed to taste
- A few drops of rosewater

Make a strong but malleable dough out of the flour, eggs, sugar and aniseed. You may need more flour to achieve the right consistency. Form small knots (pretzel shapes work well) and stick the ends together with a little rosewater. Put them into boiling water. Scoop them out when they float to the surface and allow them to dry on some kitchen towel. Place them onto a greased baking tray and bake them at a fairly low temperature until they turn golden brown. You may turn them over frequently to speed up the process which might take up to one hour.

Additional information

Tudor eggs were smaller than our modern ones but still, hardly anybody will want to make a hundred jumbals in one go. One peck equals 12½lb.

Jumbals are an iconic Tudor biscuit spiced with aniseed and typically cooked twice. These double-cooked early biscuits are from the group known as bisket. Biskets were made without yeast or salt and were considered 'slowe of dygsetyon, but it doth nouryssche moche yf it be truly ordered and well baken'. They are rather hard and therefore shapes likes pretzels work as they are easier to bite into. This type of biscuit keeps really well, and they can be frozen too.

From the early-sixteenth century finer varieties of biscuits were developed for feasts and banquets with their textures and flavours being improved by the addition of sugar, eggs, almonds, spices and rosewater. These ingredients made biscuits a very expensive type of sweetmeat and it became necessary to store them in square latten boxes with a padlock.

Anise seeds are hot and dry in the third degree says Sir Thomas Elyot in his book *The Castel of Helth.* In 1584 Thomas Cogan states that this herb is little used, but the seeds are eaten whole or made into powder. They are used to make comfits and can be easily mixed into dough.

TO MAKE MARMALAD OF QUINCES

Transcribed original recipe

> After that your Quinces are sodden, ready to be kept condict as before in the chapter is written, then with some of the liquor wherf thei were sodden (but without ani spice) beate them and drawe them as ye wolde do a Tarte, then ut some ouer the fyre to seethe softlye, and in the seething strew by little & little of

pouder of suger, ye waight of the Quinces, or more, as your
tast shall tel you, stir it continually, put ther to some pure
rosewater, or damask water, let it seeth on height til it be wal
standing some of it vpon a colde knife and let it keele, if it
bee stiff, then take it off & boxe it while it is warme, and set
it in a warm and dry ayre, yf you wyl gylde your Marmalade,
do as afore is spoken of a Marchpane. The beste making of
Marmalade is when the Quinces haue layne long & are through
ripe, And forasmuch as Quinces are bynding, and therefore not
good for some sickefolkes costife, it is necessary to put a good
may of ripe apples of good verdue, as Renet, Pyppen, Lording,
Ruussetyng, Pomeriall, Rex pomoru, or any other apple that
is pleasant raw among them, being first drawne, for a tart and
sodden amonge the other matter of Quinces. Thus shall you
make your Marmalade some what souple, and also increase the
quantitie and verdue of the same, specially if it be well dashed
with swete water.

The Treasurie of Commodious Conceits, 1573

Modernised recipe

- Quinces, pre-cooked, peeled and cored
- Sugar, same weight as quinces
- Rosewater, a few drops
- Camembert-type cheese box (not the cheese)
- Foil to line the box
- Edible gold (optional)

Put your pre-cooked, soft, peeled and cored quinces in a pan and mash them with a little water (if necessary). Weigh the quinces and add the same quantity of sugar to them in a pot. Allow them to boil but stir continuously to prevent the mixture from burning at the bottom of the pan. Add a few drops of rosewater. Continue to stir over the heat until the mixture takes on a very stiff texture. Allow mixture to cool slightly and then pour into a foil lined wooden box. Allow the marmalade to set and dry in a warm place (but not in the oven) – near a radiator would be perfect. The drying process may take weeks. The marmalade is ready for closing when the mixture feels dry and no longer sticky to the touch. If you wish to add extra lavishness, you may follow the recipe and gild your marmalade by applying edible gold.

Additional information

Tudor marmalade was a key dish in any banquet but was more like fruit leather in consistency and too solid to be spread. Indeed, it could be picked up with one's fingers, cut into bite-size squares or eaten with special sucket-forks. The name originates from the Portuguese *marmelada* (*marmelo* means quince) an imported quince paste, which was first imported into England at the end of the fifteenth century. Marmalade belonged to a group of banquet food known as dry suckets.

The preface of John Partridge's recipe book *The Treasurie of Commodious Conceits* from 1584 includes this poem mentioning the highly esteemed marmalade:

Good Huswives here you have a Jewell for your joy,
A Closet meete your huswivery to practice and imploy.
As well the gentles of degree, as eke the meaner sort,
May practice here to purchase helth, their household to co(m)fort ...
Therefore good Huswives once againe, I say to you: repayre,

Unto this loset when you neede, & mark what ye find there.
Which is a mean to make most things, to huswives use pertain
As al Conserves and Sirops sweet no comfort heart and braine.
For ba(n)quets to, here may you find, your dishes how to frame:
As Succad, *marmalade*, Marchpane to, & ech thing els by name …
Thus to co(n)clude, I wish you mark, the benefits of this booke.
Both Gentles state, the Farmers wife, & crafts mans huswife Cooke.
And if we reape commoditie by this my friends advice.
Then give him thankes, and thinke not muche, of foure pence for
the price.[11]

In 1577, William Harrison, expressed horror at outlandish feasts popular in merchants' households which included marmalades.[12] In *Health's Improvement* Thomas Muffet recommends quince marmalade for wholesome and good nourishment, especially after a meal.

Marmalade made the perfect posh food-gift, and the account books of the nobility and royalty are full of entries for it being given or received. Almost every year Elizabeth I received marmalade as a New Year's gift. In 1575 she received marmalade by Hampton, which she instantly gifted afterwards to Mrs Skydmore.[13] What an instant means of recycling unwanted gifts! Her father, Henry VIII, was clearly a lot more appreciative and rewarded James Hubert 20s for bringing marmalade to the king at York place on 19 March 1531.[14]

Marmalade made also the perfect bribe – at the Assizes in Launceston in 1599 the judges accepted one box of marmalade from Mr Wray amongst a whole list of other foods.[15]

TO CONFIT ORANGE PEELS, WHICH MAY BE DONE AT ALL TIMES IN THE YEAR AND CHIEFLY IN MAY, BECAUSE THEN THE SAID PEELS BE GREATEST AND THICKEST

Transcribed original recipe text

Take thicke Orenge péeles and them cut in foure or fiue péeces and steepe them in water the space of ten or twelue daies. You may know when they be stéeped enough, if you holde them vp in the sunne and sée through them, then they be steeped enough, & you cannot sée through them, then let them stéepe vntil you

may. Then lay them to drye vpon a table, and put them to dry betwéen two linnen clothes, then put them in a Kettell or vessel leaded, and adde to it as much Honny as will halfe couer the saide peeles, more or lesse as you think good, boyle them a little and stirre them alwaies, then take them from the fire, least the Honny should séethe ouermuch. For it should boyle a little more than it ought to boyle, it would be thick. Let it thē stand and rest foure daies in the said Honny, stirring and mingling the Orrenge and Honny euery day together. Because there is not honny enough to couer all the saide Orrenge péeles, you must stir them well and oftentimes, thus doo thrée times, giuing them one bobling at ech time, then let thē stand thrée dayes then strain them from the honny, and after you haue let them boile a small space, take them the fier, and bestow them in vessels, putting to them Ginger, cloues, and Sinamon, mix all together, and the rest of the Sirrope will serue to dresse others withal

The Good Husvvieus Iewell, 1596/7

Modernised recipe

- ◆ A number of Seville oranges
- ◆ Honey, enough to cover the boiled orange peels
- ◆ Ground ginger, ground cinnamon, and ground cloves to taste

Halve your oranges and press out the juice (Keep for other recipes). Remove all flesh and cut the peel into two halves or smaller pieces if you prefer. Boil them in water for about half an hour before changing the water. Repeat this process until the peels are beginning to appear a kind of translucent, which may require a number of changes of water and a few hours of boiling. Once this effect is achieved, remove them from the water and allow them to drain and dry on a kitchen towel. Put the dry peels into a pot and cover them with enough honey so that at least the bottom half is submerged. Allow the honey to boil – peel mixture on medium heat for a few minutes and then remove from the heat. Carefully mix, making sure all pieces have been layered with honey. Allow the mixture to boil up and then rest for three days, mixing it through daily. On day four, add the spices and mix through. Either put into jam jars for later use (I keep mine the fridge) or serve up as a dessert! The peels keep for years, if they remain completely submerged in honey which acts as the preservative.

Additional information

This is the kind of dish, sometimes also called succade, the Tudors referred to as a wet sucket. It was consumed with small, sucket forks (see photograph) and was served at banquets as a sweet treat. This is a time-consuming treat to make but definitely worth the effort. This particular recipe is interesting as it still uses honey instead of sugar.

Suckets were expensive confections, edible markers of social distinction.

In Tudor England it was fairly easy to purchase oranges if you had money. The most common one was the sour Seville type; the sweet orange only started to make an appearance in England towards the end of the sixteenth century. It came from China via Portugal and was therefore sometimes referred to as the Portuguese orange. Oranges could be purchased from specialist food markets, shops or in London also from street vendors.

As a typical 'upper-middling gentry' family the Newdigates purchased oranges as well as ready-made candied oranges quite frequently and paid up to 2s 6d and 5s for the latter.[16]

In 1591 alien John Deboyse was charged import tax for eight 'barrelles of orengys' by John Purton, Collector for the 'Custome of Stanngers goodes or marchandyse brought to the Cytie of Norwich'.[17]

Various merchants' companies show purchases of oranges for their annual feasts such as the *Dinner Book of the London Drapers' company* shows: a purchase of oranges of the value of 6d for the second Quarter Dinner held on the twenty-eighth day of May 1566.[18]

Thomas Cromwell's personal accounts from 1537 show a reward of 2s for John Freeman's servant for bringing oranges on the tenth February.[19]

On the eleventh of February 1537, Lord Lisle's neighbour, Oudart du Bies, thanks him in a letter for the oranges that 'his Lady your good bedfellow hath sent him'.[20]

Robert Dudley, Earl of Leicester's account books feature numerous entries for oranges, marmalade and suckets, most likely made of oranges, such as the entry for 7s spent on such delicacies for the year 1558/9.[21]

Elizabeth's New Year's gift exchanges are a good indication of her reputation of having a bit of a sweet tooth, in particular for orange-based treats. There are numerous entries for oranges given to her by her staff and members of the court. In 1559 gentlewoman Anes Bylliarde brought a barrel of oranges and in 1598 both her 'sargeaunts' of the 'Paystrye' gifted her a pie of 'Oringado'.[22]

Henry VIII was always the one to receive the most expensive and best food gifts. No costs were spared for him and the reward for bringing him sweet oranges and treats made from them were well rewarded. On 12 February 1531 his fruit merchant was rewarded 20s for bringing 'oreng lymmons' and marmalade to the king.[23]

Fruit sceptic Andrew Boorde surprises us with a very positive analyses of the benefits of oranges, their peel and confections made from it in his book *A Dyetary of Helth* (1542). His contemporary Sir Thomas Elyot is a little more cautious and calls for moderation. Thomas Cogan points out that the orange peel has different humoral qualities to the juice in his book *The Haven of Health*. The juice is cold in the second degree and dry in the first, but orange peel is hot in the first and dry in the second degree. In 1599 priest and academic Henry Butts recommends candied orange peel specifically for the elderly – perhaps another reason why the queen was showered with them for New Year.

CRABE OR LOPSTER

Transcribed original recipe

> To dight crabe or lopster tak crabe or lopster and stop hym at the
> vent with one of the litille clees and seethe hym in clene water or

els stop hym in the same manner and cast hym in an ovene and let hym bak and serue it with vinegar.

A Noble Boke off Cookry ffor a Prynce Houssolde, c.1480-1500

Modernised recipe

- ◆ One lobster
- ◆ Vinegar

This is the instruction for how to prepare and cook the lobster but as it does not use any other ingredients, it does not really feel like a recipe. These days, you buy a lobster already pre-cooked and so all those steps described above do not apply in the twenty-first century. The 'recipe' however states, that the crab flesh was dunked in vinegar before eaten.

Additional information

Lobsters were caught in the coastal waters of the North Sea; the season for lobsters runs from mid-March to mid-July. From *The Boke of Keruynge*, published by Wynyn de Worde in 1508, we know that the process of 'carving' a lobster was known as 'to barb'.[24]

Lobster was considered elegant and upper-class food, especially for couples due to its aphrodisiac associations. They appear to also have worked well as a bribe for corrupt judges. The list of 'gifts' given to Thomas Walmsley and Edward Fenner, two country gentlemen judges', includes lobsters received in 1596. The judges and their officers at Dorchester Assizes also received five lobsters on 13 June 1597.[25]

William Harrison, in his *The Description of England* from 1587, admits that he had never seen a lobster but goes on to explain that the river crayfish was plentiful.[26] At Kenning Hall in Norfolk, Lord Thomas Howard's home, river crayfish was preferred over lobster and the accounts for 1525 show 3d being paid for one.[27] In 1584 Thomas Cogan states in *The Haven of Health* that crab and lobster are of the same nature: very nourishing but hard to digest.

Thomas Muffet describes the flesh of lobster strong and hard. He does not give it much credit, calls it little worth. He states that lobster is best served with clove vinegar and pink flower vinegar, but it also works buttered after being well cooked in vinegar and pepper.

TO DRESSE CRABS (CREUISSES)

Translated, original recipe

> (To make Creuisses full of compound meat) Dresse them as aforesaid, and open their belly cunningly with a knife betwixt their legges, and take out all the meate out of their bellies, tailes and féet, which done, stamp it with Almonds, Currans, and yolkes of Egges, according to the quantity you will make with some cheese, Persely, and Margerum, stamped small together, and with this compound fill the Creuishes again, & séeth them again in good oyle, as softly as you may: if it bee Lent adde no Egges nor Chéefe. And if you wil fill them with variety, take Almonds stamped with Sugar and rosewater, and fill the féet with one kind, and other parts with another kind of meat.

Epulario, English translation, 1598

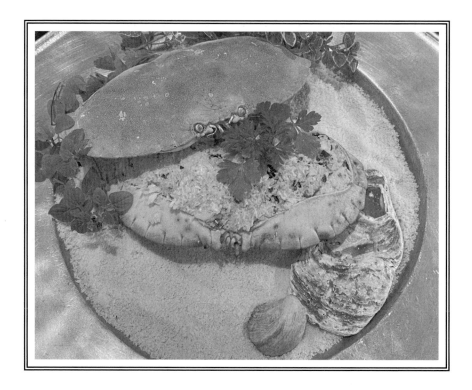

Modernised recipe

- ♦ One fresh crab (meat removed and finely chopped) – shell cleaned
- ♦ About one handful of ground almonds
- ♦ Currants, to taste
- ♦ 1-2 egg yolks, hard boiled and chopped
- ♦ Ground parmesan cheese, to taste
- ♦ Fresh parsley and marjoram, finely chopped, to taste

Mix together all the ingredients and fill the shell with mixture. If you wish, you may also fill the leg parts with a mixture of ground almonds, sugar and rosewater. The recipe suggests heating the filled crab shell in hot oil, but I would advise to briefly put it into the oven to achieve the same, possibly sprinkle some oil on top or follow the English way and use breadcrumbs instead.

Additional information

Most English recipes from this period advise crab to be eaten with vinegar, cinnamon and ginger. I chose this recipe because it illustrates how much more sophisticated the Italian way of cooking was at the time. The fact that this cookery book was translated into English as early as 1598 proves that the English nobility were ready for some Mediterranean twists. One such culinary touch was cooking with cheese such as parmesan. Indeed, in August 1511 young Henry received one hundred parmesan cheeses from the Pope in the hope of getting some much-desired English tin for St Peter's church in Rome in exchange.[28]

All recipes suggest removing the meat, chopping it and then to return it back into the shell, ready to be served. This process of being chopped up was referred to as 'taming a crab'.

Wynkin de Worde suggests in his *The Boke of Keruynge* (1508) to cover the crab with breadcrumbs, heat it and then serve it. The instructions in *Epulario* simply read 'Do as I haue said of creuisse, and eat them with vinegar'.

Thomas Muffet highly recommends crabs and advises to boil them in salted water, wine or vinegar and thinks that female crabs are better. He states that crab is best in season in the spring and autumn as well as at full moon. In 1599 Henry Butts suggests quickly roasting them on the embers and then eating them with vinegar and pepper. He ascribes them cold in second and moist in first degree.

Crab also happened to be a popular way to 'gift' – bribe a judge of the assizes. At the Assizes at Chard on 2 March 1597 one crab amongst other food gifts was presented by Mr Thomas.[29] Henry VIII paid 'Wodall's' servant a healthy 10s for bringing 'crabbes' to the king on 28 May 1530.[6] The king must really have liked them.[30]

TO MAKE IPOCRAS

Transcribed original recipe

To make Ipocras. Take of chosen Sinamon two ounces, of fine Ginger one ounce, of Graines halfe an ounce of Nutmegs halfe an pintes of good odifferous wine with a pound of Sugar, by the space of four and twenty hours: then put them into an Ipocras bag of woolen, and so receive the liquor. The readiest and best way is to put the spices with the pound of Sugar, add the wine into a bottell, or a stone pot stopped close, and after xxiiii hours it will be ready, then cast a thin linen cloth, and letting so much runthrough as ye will occupie at once, and keep the vessel close,

for it will so well keep both the spirite, odour, and virtue of the wine and also spices.

The Good Huswifes Handmaide for the Kitchin, 1594

Modernised recipe

- ◆ Pint of sweet red wine
- ◆ Approx. 1lb/450g sugar
- ◆ Ground cinnamon, ground ginger, stamped grains of paradise, ground nutmeg to taste but use it very liberally as the original recipe uses a lot! (very wasteful too)

Fill the wine into a large vessel which can be closed. Add all the spices and the sugar. Close and leave to stand for 24 hours. Drain the spices using a coffee filter. Enjoy straight away or keep in a closed bottle.

This is a very strong hypocras but lovely. Note the old way of saying 'four and twenty' instead of twenty-four, like the 'four and twenty' blackbirds in the pie!

Most recipes call for red wine, but Thomas Dawson published one for white wine: 'To make Hypocrace' in *The good Husvviues Iewell* from 1596. Elizabethan physician Thomas Cogan also gives a recipe for white 'Hipocras' in his *The Haven of Health* from 1584 (chapter 228).

Additional information

Hippocras is a high-status spiced wine often used for ceremonial purposes which was traditionally served warm or cold at the end of a meal after the table had been cleared (*void*) to aid digestion and was often served with thin wafers.

Although hippocras could be purchased, it was usually home-made just before consumption, various combinations of spices being infused in either red or white wine for up to four days, then carefully filtered to clarity by being passed through one or more conical flannel filter bags.

At Hampton Court, hippocras was made in the privy cellar. For small quantities, the spices were put into a conical filter bag of felted woollen cloth – its shape supposedly resembled the sleeves of Hippocrates, the celebrated Greek physician. A pint of wine was poured into the bag, followed by a pint of sweetened wine – then it was all poured back through the bag until it ran perfectly clear. For larger batches, beaten spices would be mixed in a gallon of wine in a pewter basin and a sample run through the first two filter bags in a row of six suspended from a bar; then the spicing of the main batch would be corrected as necessary and the whole batch passed through all six filters, after which it was poured into a vessel and sealed down until ready for use.[31]

Accounts and household books frequently list entries for hippocras. The *Dinner book of the London Draper's Company* (1564-1602) shows vast amounts being consumed at the feast dinner in August 1564: 14 gallons and a pottle at £4 in total.[32]

Hippocras also appears in the New Year gift exchanges of Elizabeth I. In 1564 she received a 'Bottell of Ipocras' from the 'Gardener Serjaunte' and again in 1598 two 'bottells' from Mr George Ducke, 'sereant of the cellar.[33]

John Smyth, a successful merchant who owned his own ship and was twice mayor of Bristol in the late-sixteenth century, wrote a recipe for hippocras listing all its ingredients in his ledger.[34]

The Norwich Chamberlains' Accounts show several entries for the purchase of hippocras. The justices of assizes paid 8s for two gallons of 'ipocras' in 1539 and 6d to Master Sall for making the hippocras.[35]

TO MAKE WAFERS

Transcribed original recipe

> Take a pinte of flowr, put it into a little creame with two yolkes
> of egges and a little rosevvater, vvith a little scarced cinamon

and sugar, vvorke them altogether and bake the paste vppon hote Irons.

Delightes for Ladies, 1602, Sir Hugh Plat

Modernised recipe

- ◆ 2 cups of flour
- ◆ 2 egg yolks
- ◆ 1tbsp of sugar
- ◆ Approx. ½- ¾ cup of cream
- ◆ Ground cinnamon to taste
- ◆ A few drops of rosewater

Mix all the ingredients and allow the mixture to stand for about 10 minutes. The wafers are made by pouring a small pool of batter onto one flat, round face of a pair of hot iron wafer-tongs. As the faces are clamped close together, the batter expands rapidly, sending spurs of surplus mixture and jets of steam from their perimeter. Once cooked to a deep cream colour, the tongs are opened and the wafer removed. After drying out briefly, wafers are then stored in closed containers for they soon become soggy, absorbing the moisture from the air.

Additional information

Wafers were made by confectioners and served with spiced wines (hippocras, clarrey) at the close of meals, but requiring no further preparation and being of high status, they were ideal for more intimate entertainment in the chambers. In fine weather they were also served in bowers, arbours or banqueting houses – luxurious summer houses erected in parks or gardens a short distance from the main residence.

Wafers could be bought ready-made from confectioner shops. In 1539 the justices of assises paid 2s 2s 'ffor too pottes off waffers'. These were probably stamped with the arms of the city.[36] The London Drapers' Company ordered eleven boxes of wafers in white, green, yellow, red and crimson for 22s from James Wharton for their feast dinner on the first Monday in August 1565.[37] 'Waffers & Hippocras' are listed in the household accounts of 1525 at Kenninghall Palace in Norfolk, the home of the Duke of Norfolk.[38]

Brigitte Webster, with kind permission by Exeter Cathedral

213

There are several medieval English recipes for wafers, but one describes a batter made of flour, egg whites, sugar, ground ginger, mixed with soft cheese and the ground stomach of a pike! I can attest that you can make them without the 'fishy bits' but you will need an early wafer iron which do sometimes turn up at auction or even in antique shops, so keep looking!

Sadly, not many original wafer ovens have survived. There is one fourteenth-century prime example at the cathedral in Exeter. This wafer oven was used for making the host wafer, the sacramental unleavened wafer bread from the Latin '*hostia*' meaning sacramental victim.

In 1584 Thomas Cogan comments in *The Haven of Health* that Galen called all kinds of unleavened bread 'unwholesome', but he excludes cakes, simnels, cracknels, buns, fritters, pancakes and wafers made from wheat 'flowre' from his harsh product rating.

TO MAKE A BUTTER PASTE (1)

Take floure, and seuer or eight egges, and cold butter & faire water, or Rosewater, and spices (if you will) & make your paste and beat it on a boorde, and when you haue so done, deuide it into two or three partes, and driue out the peece with a row ling Pinne, and doe with butter one peece by another, and then folde vp your paste vppon the butter and driue it out againe. And so doe fiue or six times together, and some not cut for bearings, and put them into the Ouen, and when they be baked, scrape suger on them, and serue them.

The Second Part of the Good Hus-wiues Iewell, 1597, Thomas Dawson

Modernised recipe

- ◆ 450g plain flour
- ◆ 150g butter
- ◆ 1 egg beaten
- ◆ 5-6 tbsp cold water with a few drops of rosewater
- ◆ Spices (optional: saffron, sugar, cinnamon)

Rub the butter into the flour and then work in the egg and water to form a stiff paste. Light kneading on a cold surface.

Additional information

During the sixteenth century we see a major change take place in the way people consumed their pies. In the beginning, the so-called 'coffin', made from flour and water only, was merely used as a convenient cooking vessel, not intended to be eaten as part of the dish and often disposed of or given to the poor. By the time Elizabeth became queen the pie pastry had been improved by adding butter and eggs, making the pie crust edible. It is around that time too, that the term 'coffin' starts to disappear from the culinary language. This transformation makes it sometimes hard to tell whether the pie crust was the earlier type or the much more desirable 'fine paste' (pastry). Unless the recipe uses butter and/or eggs for the paste or uses the term 'fine paste' you are free to choose which one you go for.

TO MAKE FINE PASTE (2)

Take faire flower and wheate, & the yolkes of egges with sweet Butter, melted, mixing all these together with your hands, til it be brought dow paste, & then make your coffins whether it be for pyes or tartes, then you may put Saffron and suger if you wil haue it a sweet paste, hauing respect to the true seasoning some vse to put to their paste Béefe or Mutton broth, and some Creame.

The Second Part of the Good Hus-wiues Iewell, 1597, Thomas Dawson

Modernised recipe

- ◆ 450g plain flour
- ◆ 250ml boiling water or beef broth
- ◆ 75g butter
- ◆ 2 egg yolks
- ◆ Pinch of crushed saffron (optional)
- ◆ 2 tbsp sugar (optional)
- ◆ 2 tbsp cream (optional)

Put your flour into a big bowl and add the yolks. Rub them into the flour until absorbed. Boil the water and melt the butter in the water. Form a well in your flour/egg mixture and pour the hot water with the melted butter into the center, mix and knead to a smooth paste.

OTHER PASTES (3)

Early paste for coffins

450g flour and 300ml boiling hot water.

Make a well in the flour, pour in water, mix with a spoon until water cools down enough to knead the dough until smooth.

Paste for Venison Pasties

450g wholewheat flour or rye flour and 240ml cold water.

Make a well in the flour, pour in cold water, mix in and knead into a smooth paste.

SOURCES

The full citation of a source is given the first time it is being used, thereafter only the author's name and publishing date.

All recipes were sourced from primary material or the following (online) transcriptions

A.W., *A Book of Cookrye*, (London: Edward Allde, 1591), Early English Books Online Text Creation Partnership, 2011, http://name.umdl.umich.edu/A14584.0001.001, accessed 17/03/2021

Dawson, Thomas, *The Good Huswwifes Iewell*, 1596, transcribed by Daniel Myers, 2008, www.medievalcookery.com/, accessed 04/02/2022

Dawson, Thomas, *The Second Part of the Good Hus-wiues Jewell*, (London: Edward Allde, 1597), Early English Books Online Text Creation Partnership, 2011,
http://name.umdl.umich.edu/A69185.0001.001, accessed 17/03/2021

Gentyll manly Cokere, MS Pepys 1047, edited as *Stere htt well* by G.A.J. Hodgett, (Cornmarket Reprints, 1972)

The Good Huswifes Handmaide for the Kitchin, 1594, (edited by Stuart Peachey, Stuart Press, 1992)

The Good Hous-wiues Treasurie, (London: Edward Allde, 1588), Early English Books Online Text Creation Partnership, 2011, http://name.umdl.umich.edu/A03731.0001.001, accessed 17/03/21

Fettiplace, Elinor, *Receipt Book*, 1647, edited by Hilary Spurling (Penguin Books, 1986)

A Noble Book off Cookry ffor a Prynce houssolde, circa 1485-1500, MS 674 (by permission of the Earl of Leicester and the Trustees of Holkkam Estate)

Partridge, J. *The Treasurie of Commodious Conceits* 1573, edited by Holloway, Johnna (2010) http://www.medievalcookery.com/notes/treasurie.pdf,

Partridge, J. *The VVidowes Treasure*, (London: Edward Alde,1588). Early English Books Online Text Creation Partnership, 2011, http://name.umdl.umich.edu/A09123.0001.001, accessed 17/03/2021

Plat, Hugh, Sir, *Delightes for ladies*, London: Peter Short, 1602, Early English Books Online Text Creation Partnership, 2011, http://name.umdl.umich.edu/A09713.0001.001, accessed 05/02/22

A Proper Newe Booke of Cokerye, 1545, edited by Hugget, Jane (Stuart Press, 1995)

Rosselli, Giovanne, de, *Epulario*, (London: A for William Barley, 1598), Early English Books Online Text Creation Partnership, 2011, http://name.umdl.umich.edu/A00309.0001.001, accessed 03/05/2021

Appriviations

TDBotLDC: *The Dinner Book of the London Drapers' Company 1564-1602, edited by Milne, S. A.* (London Record Society, 2018/9)

TPPEoKHVIII: *The Privy Purse Expenses of King Henry VIII from November 1529 to December 1532,* edited by Nicholas Harris Nicolas, 2018, (Reproduction of original by Outlook Verlag GmbH)

TENYGE: *The Elizabethan New Year's Gift Exchanges 1559-1603*, Edited by Lawson, J., (Oxford University Press, 2013)

THAoKPN: *The Household Accounts of Kenninghall Palace*, Norfolk in the year of 1525, Norfolk & Norwich Archaeological Society Vol. 15, Part1, 1902

HaadboRDEoL: *Household accounts and disbursement books of Robert Dudley, Earl of Leicester, 1558-61, 1584-86*, edited by Simon Adams (Cambridge University Press, 1995)

THotJoARtWaOC: *The Expenses of the Judges of Assize Riding the Western and Oxford Circuits*, Temp. Elizabeth, 1596-160, edited by W. Durrant Cooper, F.S.A, Camden Society)

TNAotCoSGaM: *The Norwich Accounts for the Customs on Strangers' Goods and Merchandise 1582-1610*, (Norfolk Record Society, 1970)

TNCA: *The Norwich Chamberlains' Accounts 1539-40 to 1544-5* edited by C Rawcliffe (Norfolk Record Society, Volume LXXXIII, 2019)

TroTP: *The register of Thetford Priory 1518-1540*, edited by David Dymond (Norfolk Record Society 1996)

Digital copies of primary work frequently mentioned

Butts, H., *Dyets Dry Dinner*, 1599 (http://name.umdl.umich.edu/A17373.0001.001) accessed on 5/02/22

Cogan, T., *The Haven of Health*, 1584 (http://name.umdl.umich.edu/A19070.0001.001) accessed on 05/02/22

Elyot, Thomas, *The Castel of helth* (1539) (https://quod.lib.umich.edu/e/eebo/A69278.0001.001/1:6?rgn=div Second Boke, accessed on 13/03/22

Muffet, T., *Healths Improvement*, 1655 (http://name.umdl.umich.edu/A89219.0001.001) accessed on 06/02/22 or https://quod.lib.umich.edu/cgi/t/text/text-idx?c=eebo;idno=A89219.0001.001

Reprints and facsimiles frequently mentioned

Boorde, A., *A Dyetary of Helth*, 1542, edited by Furnivall, F.J. (Adamant Media Corporation, 2005)

Gerard, J., *The Generall Historie of Plantes* 1597/1633, author's own

Harrison, W., *The Description of England*, 1587, edited by Edelen G, (Folger Shakespeare Library, 1994)

Machyn, H, *The Diary of Henry Machyn* 1550-63 edited by John Gough Nichols (Reprint, 1848)

Norwich Cathedral Priory Gardeners' accounts 1329-1530, edited by Noble, C, MA (Norfolk Record Society Volume LXI for 1997

Turner, W., *The Names of Herbes*, 1548 (Facsimile, The Ray Society, 1965)

Treveris, P., *The Grete Herball*, 1529, Facsimile

Tusser, T., *Five hundred points of good husbandry*, 1557, edited by Mavor, W, F. (Cambridge University Press, 2013)

Wynkyn de Worde, *The Boke of Keruynge*, 1508, (Reprint Equinox Publishing Ltd, 2019)

The Lisle Letters, edited by St. Clare Byrne, M (University of Chicago Press, 1983)

ENDNOTES

Introduction

1. Cogan, chapter 211, p214-20
2. Muffet, chapter XXXI, p290-95
3. Ibid. chapter XXXI, p296
4. Cogan, 1584, chapter 211, p214-220
5. Notaker, Henry, *Printed Cookbooks in Europe*, 1470-1700 (HES & DE GRAAF Publishers, 2010) p56

Chapter 1

1. Cogan, p204
2. Elyot, chapter 24, p40
3. Cogan, p136
4. Harrison, p317
5. Cogan, p132
6. *The Dinner Book of the London Drapers' Company 1564-1602,* edited by Milne, S. A. (London Record Society, 2018/9), *p*4 & 32
7. Boorde, p271
8. Muffet, p59
9. Butts
10. Cogan, p135
11. Harrison, p311
12. Muffet
13. *The Good Huswifes Handmaide for the Kitchin* 1594 (Stuart Press, 1992) p49
14. TPPEoKHVIII, p61
15. Lloyd, P. S., *Food and Identity in England* (Bloomsbury, 2015), p108
16. TDBotLDC p6, 12, 35, 49,
17. Harrison, p126
18. Thirsk, J, *Food in Early Modern England*, Continuum Books, London, 2006, p22

19. Albala, K., *Eating Right in the Renaissance* (University of California Press, 2002) p105
20. Muffet, p132 &133
21. TNAotCoSGaM, 91& 111
22. Albala, K., *A cultural history of food in the Renaissance* (Bloomsbury, 2012) p89
23. Emmison, F.G., *Wills of Essex gentry & Yeomen*, (Essex Record Office, 1980) p30
24. HaadboRDEoL p53
25. Angus, C., *My Hearty Commendations* (Caroline Angus, 2021) p256
26. St.Clare Byrne, M., *Lisle Letters* (University of Chicago Press, 1983) p143
27. TPPEoKHVIII, p66
28. THotJoARtWaOC, p46
29. Thirsk, p39
30. Harrison, p144
31. Cogan
32. Muffet, p129-131
33. TNAotCoSGaM p91
34. Emmison, p131
35. Cogan, p176 (Chapter 194)
36. TDBotLDC, p74
37. TDBotLDC, p18 & 74
38. TroTP, p746-7
39. TDBotLDC, p114
40. Angus, p354
41. Hutton, R., *The Stations of the Sun* (Oxford University Press, 1996) p152
42. Gerard, p1421
43. Breverton, T., *The Tudor Kitchen* (Amberley, 2015) p266-7
44. Hutton, p182
45. HaadboRDEoL, p62-63, & 64-65
46. Tusser, p119
47. Gerard, p650
48. TDBotLDC, p17
49. Cogan, p183-185
50. Angus, p256
51. Russel, J., *Book of Nurture in Babees Book* (James Furnivall 1868 vol. 1)
52. Albala, K., *Food in Early Modern Europe* (Greenwood Press, 2003) p71
53. Thirsk, p71
54. Ibid. p23
55. Albala, K., p105

56. Harrison, p133
57. Lloyd, p88 & 138

Chapter 2

1. Elyot, chapter 24
2. Cogan, chapter 207
3. Boorde
4. Tusser, p118
5. HaadboRDEoL, p62-65
6. Partridge, J. *The Treasurie of commodious Conceits* 1573, edited by Holloway Johnna 2010 http://www.medievalcookery.com/notes/treasurie. pdf,
7. *The Register of Thetford Priory*, part 2 1518-1540, Oxford University Press, 1996, 477
8. THAoKPN, p56
9. Turner, p187
10. Gerard, p796, 579, & 575
11. Turner, p533
12. Thirsk, p197
13. Larkin, D., (https://blog.metmuseum.org/cloistersgardens/2012/09/07/rock-samphire/)
14. Cogan, CHAP.56 Of Capers and Sampere
15. Gerard, p255
16. Turner, p 216
17. Gerard, p330
18. Lloyd, p159
19. Ibid., p39
20. Ibid., p90
21. Harrison, p317
22. TDBotLDC, p23
23. Angus, p348
24. TPPEoKHVIII, p23
25. Butts, chapter Flesh
26. Hyman, Clariss, *A global History of Oranges* (Reaktion Books, 2013) 16, 19, 20, 21
27. Harrison, p269
28. Albala, K., *A cultural history of food in the Renaissance*, p162
29. Lloyd, p158
30. TPPEoKHVIII, p173

31. Angus, p425
32. TroTP, p477
33. HaadboRDEoL, p232
34. Sonneman T., *A global history of the lemon* (Reaktion Books, 2012) 27, 38,
35. TDBotLDC, *p*17& 49
36. Harrison, p269
37. Turner, p173
38. Laws, B., *The curious history of vegetables* (Sutton Publishing, 2004) p53
39. Tusser, p119
40. Harrison, p264
41. TDBotLDC p141
42. Partridge, J. *The Treasurie of commodious Conceits* 1573, edited by Holloway Johnna 2010 http://www.medievalcookery.com/notes/treasurie. pdf, Capter xvii, p12
43. TDBotLDC, p41
44. Angus, p291
45. HaadboRDEoL, p68
46. TPPEoKHVIII, p71
47. Gerard, p 1324
48. Turner, p180
49. TDBotLDC, p52 & p50
50. Lloyd, p65
51. HaadboRDEoL, p357
52. TPPEoKHVIII, p64
53. THotJoARtWaOC, p30
54. Harrison, p269
55. Gerard, page p1446
56. TPPEoKHVIII, p187
57. TENYGE, p176

Chapter Three

1. HaadboRDEoL p270
2. TDBotLDC p183
3. Harrison, p116
4. *Lisle Letters*, p67
5. Harrison, p133
6. Albala, K, *Eating right in the Renaissance,* (University of California Press, 2002) p59

7. Cogan, chapter 8
8. Muffet, chapter XXIV
9. Norwich Cathedral Priory, Gardener's account, p73
10. Turner, p32/174
11. Tusser, p121
12. Harrison, p264
13. Gerard, p922
14. THotJoARtWaOC, p15
15. Gerard, p1407
16. Albala, p181
17. Lloyd, p42
18. HaadboRDEoL, p247
19. TDBotLDC p32
20. THotJoARtWaOC, p30
21. De Worde W *The Boke of Keruynge* 1508, (Equinox Publishing Ltd 2019, Southover Press 2003) p16
22. Harrison, p129
23. De Worde, p15
24. Anon, *A Proper Newe Booke of Cokerye*,
25. TDBotLDC, p7
26. THotJoARtWaOC, p214
27. TDBotLDC p95
28. Gentilcore, D., *Food and Health in Early Modern Europe*, (Bloomsbury, 2016) p17
29. TPPEoKHVIII, p187
30. THAoKPN p56
31. Ibid., p56
32. *The Lisle letters*, p246
33. TPPEoKHVIII p76
34. Turner, p207
35. Gerard, p1497
36. TDBotLDC p15
37. Lloyd, p125
38. TENYGE, p176
39. Lloyd, p125
40. HaadboRDEoL, p205
41. *The Lisle Letters*, p246
42. Gerard, p1453
43. TPPEoKHVIII, p23

44. TENYGE 82,98,124,160, 215, 235,339,473.
45. TDBotLDC p113
46. Ibid., p7, 99, 107, 113
47. TPPEoKHVIII, p103
48. Gerard, p1458
49. TNCA p264
50. Angus, p290 & 353
51. TPPEoKHVIII, p 57
52. HaadboRDEoL, p44
53. TENYGE, p215
54. Roach, p 122
55. Roberts, p29
56. Ibid., p26
57. TPPEoKHVIII, p76
58. HaadboRDEoL p48
59. TNCA p45

Chapter 4

1. Harrison, p123
2. Tusser, p77
3. Hutton, p9
4. Tusser, p71
5. Weir, A and Clarke S, *A Tudor Christmas* (Penguin Random House UK, 2018), p41
6. Woolgar, C. M. *The culture of food in England* 1200-1500 (Yale University Press, 2016) p121
7. HaadboRDEoL p195, 42
8. Lloyd, p147
9. Ibid., p71
10. Harrison, p316-7
11. Lloyd, p108
12. Ibid., p64
13. Dawson, M, *Plenti and Grasse*, (Prospect Books, Totnes, 2009) p108 &110
14. Holloway, J., On Turkeys and Great Birds, 2005 (http://www.florilegium. org/) accessed 28.12.21
15. Brears, P., Cooking & Dining in Tudor & Early Stuart England (Prospect Books, 2015) p21

16. Thirsk p251-2
17. Tusser, 31. Christmas husbandlie fare, chap. 29
18. TDBotLDC 5
19. THotJoARtWaOC, p21
20. Harrison, 317
21. Brears, p21
22. THotJoARtWaOC, p21
23. Albala, K, *Food in Early Modern Europe,* p70
24. *The Lisle letters*, p206-7
25. Lloyd, p113
26. HaadboRDEoL p65, 70
27. TDBotLDC. p38
28. THotJoARtWaOC, p17
29. Worde, de Wynkyn, *The Boke of Keruynge,* 1508
30. Tilley, M., P., A Dictionary of The Proverbs in England in the sixteenth and seventeenth centuries (1950) p95
31. Winchester, B., *Tudor Family Portrait* (London, 1955) p136
32. HaadboRDEoL, 310
33. THotJoARtWaOC, p27
34. TPPEoKHVIII p145
35. Tilley, p56 (B481)
36. Albala, K, *Food in Early Modern Europe,* p69
37. TPPEoKHVIII, p201 &202
38. THotJoARtWaOC, p27
39. Angus, p353
40. HaadboRDEoL, p248
41. TENYGE p44
42. THotJoARtWaOC, p21
43. TDBotLDC, p125
44. *The Lisle Letters*, 94
45. Machyn, p208
46. Angus, p34
47. HaadboRDEoL, p300
48. THotJoARtWaOC, p31
49. Brear, p163
50. Tusser, p73
51. Harrison, 264
52. Gerard, p231
53. HaadboRDEoL, p93
54. TPPEoKHVIII, p100

55. Fettiplace, E, *Receipt Book*, 1647 (Spurling H, Penguin Books, 1986) p137 & p53
56. Hutton, p13
57. Ibid., p13
58. Brears, p85
59. Machyn, p99
60. Gerard, p1460

Chapter Five

1. *A cultural history of food in the Renaissance*, p106
2. Angus, p119
3. HaadboRDEoL p142
4. Harrison, p129
5. Machyn, p135
6. TENYGE p62
7. Ibid., p63
8. THAoKPN, p56
9. *Country and City Wymondham, Norwich and Eaton in the 16ᵗʰ & 17ᵗʰ centuries* (Norfolk Record Society, 2006) p40
10. HaadboRDEoL, p42
11. Partridge, J, The Treasurie of Commodious Conceits, 1591 (EEBO Edition)
12. Harrison, p129
13. TENYGE, p176
14. TPPEoKHVIII p107
15. THotJoARtWaOC, p34
16. Lloyd, 134
17. TNAotCoSGaM p98
18. TDBotLDC, p49
19. Angus, p289
20. *The Lisle letters*, p286
21. HaadboRDEoL, p93
22. TENYGE, p41 & 454
23. TPPEoKHVIII, p103
24. De Worde, p 26
25. Lloyd, p166, 168
26. Harrison, p323
27. THAoKPN, p56
28. *BHO, Letters and Papers*, Foreign and Domestic, Henry VIII, Volume 1, 1509-1514, ed J S Brewer (London, 1920) http://www.british-history.ac.uk/letters-papers-hen8/vol1 (accessed 23 May 2022)

29. TNAotCoSGaM, p25
30. TPPEoKHVIII:, p64
31. Brears, p413
32. TDBotLDC, *p*10
33. TENYGE, *p*98, 454
34. Lloyd., p66
35. TNCA, p82
36. Ibid., p82
37. TDBotLDC, p40
38. THAoKPN, p57

For any guidance or queries about the preparation of the dishes in this book, you are very welcome to contact me via my website www.tudorexperience. com, my Twitter account @tudorfoodrecipe, my Instagram @tudor_experience or my special Tudor food Facebook page @TUDOR Cooking, Recipes, Food & Eating.

INDEX (RECIPES)

Food and recipes (Numbers in **BOLD** indicate use in recipes.)